ARM-BALL TO ZOOTER

ARM-BALL TO ZOOTER

A SIDEWAYS LOOK AT THE LANGUAGE OF CRICKET

LAWRENCE BOOTH

Cartoonist: Nick Newman

PENGUIN BOOKS

*To Butz (1901–2006), who never quite understood,
but was always happy for me*

PENGUIN BOOKS

Published by the Penguin Group
Penguin Books Ltd, 80 Strand, London WC2R ORL, England
Penguin Group (USA) Inc., 375 Hudson Street, New York, New York 10014, USA
Penguin Group (Canada), 90 Eglinton Avenue East, Suite 700, Toronto, Ontario, Canada M4P 2Y3
(a division of Pearson Penguin Canada Inc.)
Penguin Ireland, 25 St Stephen's Green, Dublin 2, Ireland
(a division of Penguin Books Ltd)
Penguin Group (Australia), 250 Camberwell Road,
Camberwell, Victoria 3124, Australia (a division of Pearson Australia Group Pty Ltd)
Penguin Books India Pvt Ltd, 11 Community Centre,
Panchsheel Park, New Delhi – 110 017, India
Penguin Group (NZ), 67 Apollo Drive, Mairangi Bay, Auckland 1310,
New Zealand (a division of Pearson New Zealand Ltd)
Penguin Books (South Africa) (Pty) Ltd, 24 Sturdee Avenue,
Rosebank, Johannesburg 2196, South Africa

Penguin Books Ltd, Registered Offices: 80 Strand, London WC2R ORL, England

www.penguin.com

First published 2006

1

Copyright © Lawrence Booth, 2006
Illustrations copyright © Nick Newman 2006
All rights reserved

The moral right of the author has been asserted

Set in Fairfield
Typeset by Palimpsest Book Production Limited, Grangemouth, Stirlingshire
Printed in England by Clays Ltd, St Ives plc

ISBN-13: 978–0–140–51581–7
ISBN-10: 0–140–51581–X

CONTENTS

ILLUSTRATIONS

INTRODUCTION

Since I first caught the cricket bug in the late 1980s, I have been working on a stock response to the sceptics who wonder, not unreasonably when you think about it, what all the fuss is about. 'Give me an hour at a match with anyone who has even the slightest modicum of intelligence,' I say, pandering transparently to their ego, 'and I will convert them.'

It's a pathetic ruse, I'll grant you. But desperate times call for desperate measures, and – even in the afterglow of the 2005 Ashes – Britain's submissive relationship with football, a sport I once loved too, demands dirty tricks.

Very few people have ever taken me up on the offer of a mini-tutorial, citing excuses which have ranged from hair-washing to preferring the sight of drying paint. I hope this book provides a more entertaining alternative and even manages to change a few minds.

Cricket anoraks like to think that, to understand their sport, you need God-given intuition of the kind useful for getting to grips with a foreign language or an Ikea wardrobe. Yet no one, not even Richie Benaud, has ever emerged from the womb with a ready-made understanding of the lbw Law.

Everyone needs its complexities explained to them at some stage or other, and there should be no shame in this (well, not much: it really isn't that hard once you've grasped the fact that a batsman cannot be given out if the ball has pitched outside leg-stump or the umpire comes from New Zealand). Since cricket revels in its sense of order – from the batting averages calculated to two decimal places to the ritual breaks for lunch and tea – an A to Z seemed like a fitting format.

But it quickly became clear that a conventional A to Z was out of the question. I began writing with the intention of poking fun at cricket's hilarious vocabulary, but kept getting distracted by one tangent after another. A few days before writing this, for instance, I discovered that my entry on John Travolta (bear with me) had negligently overlooked the fact that Travolta is also the middle name of an international cricketer. The more distractions, the more tangled the web, and the less point there seemed in sticking to the original plan.

What has emerged is part-encyclopedia, part-guidebook, part-declaration of affection, part-repository for wanton gags. Cricket stalwarts should learn a thing or two. Cricket newcomers will finally be able to look those stalwarts in the face and explain – without hesitation, repetition or deviation – the ins and outs of a chinaman.

Well, that's the hope. Happy browsing.

Lawrence Booth
London, June 2006

BIBLIOGRAPHY

Ashes: True Tales from Cricket's Greatest Stars (London, 1991: Angus & Robertson)
Harmless fun. The perfect book for the downstairs loo – and that's a compliment.

Richie Benaud, **Anything But . . . An Autobiography** (London, 1998: Hodder & Stoughton)
Pearls of wisdom, but leaves you wanting a lot more. Perhaps the clue is in the title.

Richie Benaud, **The Appeal of Cricket** (London, 1995: Hodder & Stoughton)
Richie is a serviceable writer, but he's definitely a better broadcaster.

Rahul Bhattacharya, **Pundits from Pakistan: On Tour with India, 2003–04** (London, 2005: Picador)
A breath of fresh air in an age of ghosted tat. Inspects India's historic tour of Pakistan from several innovative angles.

Derek Birley, **A Social History of English Cricket** (London, 1999: Aurum Press)
Scholarly and fascinating. Top of the reading list if there were such a thing as a degree in cricket.

Derek Birley, **The Willow Wand: Some Cricket Myths Explored** (London, 2nd edn, 2000: Aurum Press)
Brilliantly sustained piece of iconoclasm: received wisdom is held up to the light.

Ian Botham, **Botham's Century: My 100 Great Cricketing Characters** (London, 2001: Collins Willow)

Only Botham could have got away with a book like this, but there are plenty of anecdotes to keep you amused.

Philip Brown and Lawrence Booth, **Cricket: Celebrating the Modern Game around the World** (London, 2005: Mitchell Beazley)
You'll love the pictures.

Nick Callow, **Amazing Cricket Facts** (London, 2005: Virgin)
Quirky and endearing, but – if we're honest – amazing might be stretching it.

Stephen Chalke, **Runs in the Memory** (Bath, 2002: Fairfield)
County cricket in the 1950s – Chalke does personal very, very well.

Mike Coward, **Calypso Summer** (Sydney, 2000: ABC)
An in-depth, well-illustrated rendition of the astonishing 1960–61 series between Australia and West Indies.

John Crace, **Wasim and Waqar: Imran's Inheritors** (London, 1992: Boxtree)
Published just before the pair's zenith – the 1992 tour of England – but still captures the essence of one of the game's most destructive bowling partnerships.

Ralph Dellor and Stephen Lamb, **The Little Book of Cricket: A Cricketing A to Z** (London, 2005: Green Umbrella)
Beautifully presented, but with only one entry per letter.

Rob Eastaway, **What is a Googly?** (London, new edn, 2004: Robson)
A good gift for anyone wanting to help a friend demystify cricket.

John Emburey, **Spinning in a Fast World** (London, 1989: Robson)

A brave attempt to fly the flag for slow bowlers. Workmanlike rather than sparkling.

Jack Fingleton, **Brightly Fades the Don** (London, 1949: Collins; reissued London, 1983: Pavilion)
A priceless account of Australia's 1948 tour of England, Bradman's last Test series.

David Frith, **Bodyline Autopsy: The Full Story of the Most Senational Test Cricket Series England v Australia 1932–3** (London, 2002: Aurum Press)
The definitive version of cricket's most bloodthirsty series by the game's most assiduous historian.

David Frith, **England versus Australia: A Pictorial History of Every Test Match since 1877** (London, 1997: BBC Books)
Reports and pictures. Encyclopaedic.

David Frith, **The Fast Men** (London, 1975: Corgi)
The history of fast bowling, and a riveting one too.

Ramachandra Guha (ed.), **The Picador Book of Cricket** (London, 2001: Picador)
Unputdownable collection of some of cricket writing's finest moments.

Gideon Haigh, **The Cricket War** (Melbourne, 1993: Text Publishing)
A masterclass in how to cast new light on a subject – Kerry Packer's World Series – that everyone thought they knew about already.

Andrew Hignell, **Rain Stops Play: The Geography of Cricket** (London, 2002: Cass)
It won't set the pulse racing, but you have to admire the science in this survey of the English game's geography.

Simon Hughes, **Jargonbusting: Mastering the Art of Cricket** (London, 2001: Channel 4 Books)
Typically thoughtful and helpful production by the Analyst: a great introduction to the game.

Simon Hughes, **Morning Everyone: A Sportswriter's Life** (London, 2005: Orion)
Candid, critical, lovable. Why aren't more sports books like this?

C. L. R. James, **Beyond a Boundary** (London, reprinted 1996: Serpent's Tail)
History, sociology, philosophy and cricket – the development of the West Indies seen through several, equally illuminating, prisms.

Frank Keating, **Frank Keating's Sporting Century: The Best, the Worst, the Weirdest . . .** (London, 1998: Robson)
If you can't enjoy Keating, you might as well give up on the rest of us. Lap it up.

Tony Lewis, **Double Century: Two Hundred Years of the MCC** (Kent, 1987: Hodder & Stoughton)
An admirable history by the former president of the MCC.

Dennis Lillee, **Menace: The Autobiography** (London, 2003: Headline)
Not as thought-provoking as his bowling, but all the anecdotes are here: the aluminium bat, the bet at Headingley, the set-to with Javed Miandad . . .

Kersi Meher-Homji, **The Nervous Nineties** (Kenthurst, Australia, 1994: Kangaroo Press)
A testament to the perils of approaching a century: statistical rather than poetical.

Peter Oborne, **Basil D'Oliveira. Cricket and Conspiracy: The Untold Story** (London, 2004: Time Warner)

A magnificent piece of journalism examining one of cricket's most shameful episodes.

Andrew Radd, **Northamptonshire County Cricket Club: 100 Greats** (Stroud, 2001: Tempus)
A thankless task, you might think, but Radd was probably the only man alive who could have pulled it off.

Simon Rae, **It's Not Cricket: Skulduggery, Sharp Practice and Downright Cheating in the Noble Game** (London, 2001: Faber and Faber)
A superbly researched rebuff to all those who think cricket is a gentleman's game.

K. S. Ranjitsinhji, **Jubilee Book of Cricket** (Edinburgh and London, 1897: William Blackwood and Sons)
A delightfully dated manual straight from the Golden Age, with all its airs and Graces.

David Rayvern Allen, **Arlott: The Authorised Biography** (London, 1994: HarperCollins)
Insightful, perceptive and highly readable.

Jonathan Rice, **Curiosities of Cricket** (London, 1993: Pavilion)
The kind of compendium that only cricket can inspire. For anoraks and novices alike.

Alan Ross, **Cape Summer** (London, 1957: Hamish Hamilton; reissued London, 1986: Constable)
The elegant musings of a highly gifted Sunday-newspaper journalist with all the time in the world. Covers England's tour of South Africa in 1956–57.

Rowland Ryder, **Cricket Calling** (London, 1995: Faber and Faber)
Fondly written reminiscences of a life in cricket. A gentle read.

Rob Steen (ed.), **The New Ball** (London, 1998: Two Heads)
Great read. It's just a pity Steen's laudable attempt to provide a regular forum for a more cerebral brand of cricket writing didn't last the distance.

Mark Taylor, **Time to Declare** (Sydney, 1999: Ironbark)
One of the better ghosted autobiographies, although that isn't saying much.

Graham Thorpe, **Rising from the Ashes** (London, 2005: Harper-Collins Willow)
A sportsman's private life can rarely have dominated an autobiography as much as this. This is the book's strength and its weakness.

Charles Williams, **Bradman** (London, 1996: Little, Brown)
The Don in context. Like his batting, oozes authority.

Graeme Wright (ed.), **Wisden on Bradman** (Sydney, 1999: Hardie Grant)
Two of the most thorough phenomena in cricket history team up, with predictably high-class results.

Also: **The Cricketers' Who's Who**, **The Wisden Cricketer**, **Waitrose Food Illustrated**, **Wisden Cricketers' Almanack**, **Wisden Cricket Monthly**, *www.bbc.co.uk* (Ask Bearders), *www.cricinfo.com*, *www.google.com*, *www.wikipedia.com*.

ACKNOWLEDGEMENTS

It's a perilous business trying to thank everyone who has in some way contributed to the fact that a book actually exists, but I would like to single out someone whose influence is a recurring theme in my working life. Without Tim de Lisle, who was editor of *Wisden Cricket Monthly* when I arrived for work experience in the summer of 1998, I might not have discovered the possibilities of the written word. For that I will always be grateful.

In the shorter term Jenny Thompson was a constant source of good-natured inspiration and a veritable well of word-plays, many of which must remain a secret on the grounds of taste. Michael Peel watched over me like a kindly uncle, raising his eyebrows when my attempted jokes rang alarm bells and providing stamps of approval which I cherished. My agent, Jim Gill, encouraged wholeheartedly, advised impeccably and at times alarmed me with the breadth of his knowledge on subjects he had no business to know anything about.

Georgina Laycock, my editor at Penguin, was an absolute pleasure to work with, and not only because she indulged my flights of fancy. Mark Handsley subbed with the kind of awesome precision I thought existed only in the dark recesses of *Wisden Cricketers' Almanack* (any mistakes that remain, as they always seem to say, are my own). Nick Newman's cartoons made me laugh out loud, as I knew they would. My brother Alex, who was living with me while I wrote this book, chivvied me along and knew where and when to print cheap copies of my latest draft.

Gideon Haigh, Martin Williamson, Steven Lynch and Mark Geenty were typically generous with their time and information, and I'm grateful to Mark Eklid for his rendition of the incident in which a county cricketer almost had his eye poked out by his son (see Travolta, John). Sarah Beckett was the punctuation queen *non-pareille*.

But my biggest thanks go to Fiona Learmont. For your support and attentiveness, your pep-talks and your affection, this book is for you.

Lawrence Booth
London, June 2006

ADJUDGE

A needlessly pompous word to describe what is done to batsmen who are given out LEG BEFORE WICKET (as opposed to those who are simply and indisputably *out* lbw). The reporter using 'adjudged' might well disagree with the umpire's decision but isn't brave enough to say so in print. Thus, a comment like 'Bloggs was adjudged lbw for 99 to hand the ASHES to Australia' might be written with a sly raise of the eyebrow and a shake of the head, which is precisely how you should react when reading it.

See also DISMISSALS.

AGRICULTURE

Few activities have as little in common with each other as farming (back-breaking work integral to the nation's wellbeing) and professional cricket (a self-indulgent waste of time), although a Zimbabwean chicken farmer called Eddo Brandes once humiliated England with a HAT-TRICK. And yet the agricultural SLOG is the most natural batting stroke of them all – a baseball-style heave across the line designed to scatter crowds and sicken the purists who have not quite shaken off the Victorian belief that it is bad manners to score runs on the leg-side. Appropriately enough, most agricultural shots are called mows and end up in cow corner, the usually unguarded region between deep midwicket and long-on. The cow reference is believed to have started at Dulwich College in south-east London, where livestock grazed beyond the BOUNDARY. Unkind allusions to agriculture probably wormed their way into cricket's lexicon when Australian farmers took part in city *v* country games and managed to smite the ball harder and further than their puny urban opponents. In which case its usage as a term of abuse is nothing but jealousy and snobbery.

See also FIELDING POSITIONS.

ALBANIA

The most exciting offer most cricketers get to turn down is an interview request from the local paper. C. B. Fry turned down the throne of Albania. Charles Burgess Fry (1872–1956) was the ultimate polymath: aside from playing FIRST-CLASS cricket for thirty years, in which time he AVERAGED 50 with the bat and won twenty-six Test caps, he turned out for England at FOOTBALL, the Barbarians at RUGBY, was briefly joint-holder of the world long-jump record, represented India at the League of Nations, and – in his later, less stable, years – allegedly tried to persuade Joachim von Ribbentrop, Hitler's foreign minister, that Nazi Germany should take up Test cricket. After all, their bowlers might have been a dab hand at MILITARY MEDIUM.

Not long after the First World War, the Albanian people forced out their German-born rulers, thus creating the sort of vacancy that county clubs know only too well when their best scoreboard operator is poached by a bitter local rival. Fry's friendship with his well-connected Sussex and England colleague Ranjitsinhji landed him the post of substitute delegate for India at the League of Nations in Geneva, where he wrote a speech – delivered by Ranji – which helped turf Mussolini out of Corfu. Possibly impressed by this, the Albanians sent a delegation to try to persuade Fry to take up their crown, but he declined on the grounds that he did not earn the required amount of £10,000 a year.

But the suspicion remains that Fry's heart was never really in Tirana. 'If I had really pressed Ranji to promote me,' he wrote in his autobiography, *Life Worth Living*, 'it is quite on the cards that I should have been King of Albania yesterday, if not today.' Instead, the throne was seized by the former Albanian Prime Minister, Ahmed-I-Zog, who became King Zog in 1928. He had probably never even heard of the sport, thus robbing Test cricket of a potential new addition, and England of some easy wins in the Balkans.

See also CHUCKING; GLANCE; GOLDEN AGE.

ALL-ROUNDER

A good all-rounder is a captain's dream – a master of all trades, a jack of none, and proof that two into one really does go. A bad all-rounder will take 1 for 60 from 10 overs, drop a crucial slip catch, then SLOG a quick 7 (county cricket is full of these creatures). The all-rounder's acid test is whether he would make a side purely as a batsman or a bowler. In some cases, it is passed spectacularly. Garry Sobers averaged over 57 with the bat in ninety-three

Tests for West Indies, and took 235 wickets with such a subtle mixture of left-arm seam, left-arm orthodox spin and CHINAMEN that opponents complained it was like playing against thirteen men. Keith Miller scored 2,958 runs for Australia at nearly 37, took 170 wickets at under 23, and seduced almost as many women. And Pakistan's Imran Khan averaged 19 with the ball and virtually 50 with the bat in the last ten years of his Test career.

Imran was at his peak in the 1980s, which – with apologies to W. G. GRACE – was the true GOLDEN AGE of all-rounders. India had Kapil Dev, New Zealand had Richard Hadlee, and England had Ian Botham. Each had different strengths. Imran was the classiest batsman, Hadlee the most complete bowler; Kapil showed his fellow seamers that it was possible to prosper on the subcontinent, where he took 279 of his 434 Test wickets; and Botham won matches through sheer bravado as well as being the only figure in modern civilization to leave Australians with an inferiority complex. Only he and Imran have ever scored a century and taken ten wickets in a Test.

As far as England were concerned, however, Botham was a blessing who turned into a curse, and no all-rounder who appeared for them after his international retirement in 1992 could escape the comparison. The 'new Botham' tag – more of an albatross crossed with a black cat – was affixed at various stages to Phil DeFreitas, Derek Pringle, David Capel, Chris Lewis, Dominic Cork, and the lady who made the teas at Trent Bridge. But it was not until Andrew Flintoff swapped beer for cranberry juice that a true successor was found, even if Botham might not approve of his tipple. These days, Botham's all-round skills are such that fellow Sky Sports commentators take it in turns to match him drink for drink on nights out. No, he hasn't lost it.

See also BITS AND PIECES; CHARACTER; FOLLOW-ON; INVINCIBLES; PRESSURE.

ALUMINIUM

The echoing clang of leather on aluminium is one cliché that never quite took off. On 15 December 1979 Dennis Lillee strode self-consciously out to the middle of the WACA at Perth to resume his innings of 11 in the first Test between Australia and England. He was carrying an aluminium bat, which was perfectly legal at the time, if only because no one dreamed one would ever be used. It would have been like telling players they were not allowed to dress up as chimps.

Lillee had already shown off his new toy two weeks earlier, in the Brisbane Test against West Indies. Since he had made a DUCK in that game, no one was too bothered. But when he straight-drove Ian Botham's fourth ball of the day for two, the England captain, Mike Brearley, complained that the bat was damaging the ball and refused to continue unless Lillee reverted to WILLOW. After what Lillee later described as a 'Mexican stand-off', he flounced back to the pavilion to change bats, only to re-emerge with his lump of metal following some mischievous provocation from his team-mate Rod Marsh.

It was now that the Australia captain, Greg Chappell, became involved. First he sent Rodney Hogg out with a new bat. Then, when Lillee told Hogg where to stick it, Chappell emerged himself. Lillee was so infuriated that, with all the maturity and good grace of a thirty-year-old playing his thirty-fourth Test, he hurled his bat ('the offending object' in most versions) a full thirty yards in Chappell's direction. The Australian Cricket Board let him off with a warning; a few months later a Law was passed stating that the bat had to be made 'solely of wood'. These days Lillee would have been fined half his match fee and ordered to undergo a course in anger management.

His experiment, it turned out, had not simply been in the name of science. A friend of his, Graham Monaghan, had been manufacturing aluminium bats as a cheaper alternative, and Lillee was now giving the new ComBat the best exposure possible ('I'm not ashamed of that,' he wrote in his autobiography). When he later asked the two sets of players to sign the bat, Brearley wrote: 'Good luck with the sales.' They rocketed for a while, but when the bat was banned, consumers lost interest.

Back in Perth, Lillee was eventually out for 18 (willow 15, aluminium 3), before tearing in to remove the England openers, Geoff Boycott and Derek Randall, for ducks on his way to figures of 4 for 73. Boycott later told Brearley he had made a big mistake. 'He thought it fired the great fast bowler up to an extra effort with the ball,' chuckled Brearley, who top-scored for England with 64 from the relative safety of No. 6 before Lillee had him caught behind. Australia went on to win the game and the series.

Years later came a tiny, tinny echo of the Lillee affair. Just over a month before the Australians were due to land in England for the 2005 ASHES tour, the MCC expressed concern that the bat belonging to Australia's captain, Ricky Ponting, was being unfairly strengthened by a strip of carbon graphite, which was like complaining that Jonny Wilkinson's place-kicking was being aided by the presence on his left boot of an extra stud.

A no-stone-unturned investigation was launched by the ICC, who later issued a stern statement extolling the virtues of cricket as 'a battle between a wooden bat and leather ball' and set up an 'expert panel' to look into the matter. In February 2006, they announced that the MCC, still considered the guardians of cricket's laws, had deemed the bat illegal. The manufacturers, Kookaburra, immediately agreed to withdraw all graphite-enforced bats from the international game, and the world rotated on its axis once more.

See also HELMETS; QUEEN, THE; UNDERARM BOWLING.

AMBUSH MARKETING

Dreamed up to make the corporate world sound thrill-a-minute, the phrase 'ambush marketing' has nothing whatsoever to do with middle-aged men running around in pin-stripe suits and cowboy hats screaming 'We'll head the critters off at the pass!' It is a highly petty, deeply tedious, bitterly vindictive spoiling tactic used by one multinational company to muscle into the territory of another. Example: when Coca-Cola co-sponsored the 1996 World Cup, their old chums Pepsi threw an enormous strop and filled the skies with hot-air balloons bearing their logo. Yes, they really were prepared to soar to such heights/plumb such depths in order to grab a slice of the bloated commercial pie.

Of course, the problem with ambush marketing is that tournament organizers have to take it very seriously if they are to keep their sponsors happy, or indeed keep their sponsors at all. At a warm-up game in Cape Town prior to the 2003 World Cup, the labels on the bottled water used in the hospitality suites had to be covered up with blue tape in case it offended the poor lambs at Pepsi, who by now had been allowed to join the party. And at the ICC Champions Trophy in England in 2004, spectators were not allowed to bring Coca-Cola into the ground: the sight of stewards pouring fizzy brown swill from one vessel to another was more memorable than most of the cricket. The ICC protested that they had little choice but to come over all draconian. Spectators, feeling as ambushed as the multinationals, simply shrugged their shoulders and vowed never to return. It was cricket PR at its very best.

See also PARTY, COMING TO THE; ZOOTER.

ANALYST, THE

Innovations do not always go down well in the occasionally hidebound world of cricket, so when the former Middlesex and Durham seamer Simon Hughes began providing fascinating titbits of analysis for Channel 4's new Test coverage in 1999 from the darkened recesses of a large truck, the inevitable grumbles were not far behind. Delighted cynics discovered that by subtly changing the pronunciation of the first syllable of the 'Analyst' – Hughes's new sobriquet – they could convey a less complimentary impression altogether.

The joke was as harsh as it was unfunny. Hughes's eagle eye for detail and intelligent interpretation of subjects as apparently arcane as Nasser Hussain's forward defensive and Robert Croft's ARM-BALL helped persuade a wider audience that cricket was not simply freemasonry in whites. Hughes was initially accompanied in his unglamorous truck-cum-bunker by the former Warwickshire captain Dermot Reeve. But, wrote Hughes, 'Reeve soon tired of the idea, realizing it constrained his grand ambitions involving commentary and marketing girls.' In 2005 Reeve was sacked by Channel 4 after admitting to a cocaine habit, while Hughes continued to pore diligently in the gloom over split-screens and super slo-mos. It was unclear whose health suffered more.

See also CHUCKING; DRUGS; HAWKEYE; SNICKOMETER.

ANCHOR

If you decide to anchor an innings, you are probably your side's most technically correct batsman, or at least you think you are. While your feckless team-mates blaze away at the other end, throwing caution to the wind and their wickets to the opposition, you calmly NUDGE the ones and twos, hit the very bad ball for four, and ensure in an eminently sensible, accountant-like way that there will be a decent total at the end of it all. By then you will have convinced yourself you have earned the right to feel very smug about life.

To *drop* anchor is to enter even more risk-free territory. You are not merely holding the innings together, but in all probability clogging it up. The adhesive you were hoping to provide has to your team-mates' horror – assuming any of them are still awake – turned into quick-drying cement. Anchor-droppers will always argue that their colleagues' rashness left them with little choice, in much the same way as unfaithful spouses blame their wanderings on the inattentions of their partner. Don't listen to them.

See also REARGUARD; STONEWALL.

ARM-BALL

It's easy to sneer at the arm-ball, the off-spinner's delivery that does not TURN and, given a favourable breeze, might DRIFT away from the right-handed batsman. The reason for its tendency to elicit a titter is that it has been usurped in the off-spin bowler's arsenal by the far more dangerous DOOSRA, and is usually associated with English county pros who suddenly find themselves playing a Test match in Ahmedabad or Lahore. And panicking just a little. There are some ungenerous souls who believe the arm-ball, so called because it travels straight on in the direction of the bowling arm, is simply a polite way of saying that the bowler has failed to actually spin the ball, but this would be to denigrate an entire generation of English OFF-BREAK bowlers. Then again, these ungenerous souls probably have a point.

ASHES, THE

The new breed of cricket follower might be forgiven for thinking that 'Ashes' exists only in conjunction with 'mania'. But the history of the sport extends back to an era when the summer of 2005 was barely a glint in the eye of Andrew Flintoff biographers. In 1882, Australia beat England by 7 runs at The Oval (yes, in those days, the nailbiters were occasionally won by Australia). The result

An early example of Australian sledging by Frederick 'The Demon' Spofforth

prompted a mock obituary for English cricket in the *Sporting Times*, which ended with the kind of faux solemnity rarely found in Victorian Britain: 'The body will be cremated and the ashes taken to Australia.'

When the English team, captained by Ivo Bligh (later known on the streets as the eighth Earl of Darnley), won in Australia that winter, a group of Melbourne high-society ladies burned what is generally believed to be a set of bails and, in an early example of the truism that size doesn't matter, presented the remains to Bligh in a four-inch terracotta urn. Bligh was so moved he ended up marrying one of the pranksters, Florence Morphy (in time to become the Countess of Darnley), and a legend was born.

The urn, which was bequeathed to the MCC in 1929, two years after Bligh's death, is kept in whichever country has won the most recent series – unless that team happens to be Australia, in which case it remains under lock and key in a glass case in the LORD's museum in St John's Wood, London. For years this was a source of great irritation to the Australians, especially after they won a record eight successive series between 1989 and 2002–03. But England recently ended the monopoly and the noises from Down Under suddenly disappeared.

The Ashes are played for twice every four years over series of five or six Tests, and generally appear alongside phrases such as 'unique tradition', 'love–hate relationship', and 'no quarter asked nor given'. In reality, they simply determine bragging-rights in the pubs and clubs of south-west London, where Australian barmen are rumoured to have spiked their English customers' wine with Foster's lager in retaliation for losing a Test. The English, on the other hand, pretend to be above it all when they suffer defeat, only to lose all sense of proportion when they win. Rolf Harris, the cast of *Neighbours* and Kwickie Koala have rarely taken such a pummelling at the hands of the British red-tops as they did in 2005.

It is perhaps just as well, then, that English victories have been outnumbered by English defeats: before the 2006–07 series, Australia lead both in terms of Ashes Tests won (117 to 95) and series in possession of the urn (34 to 29). Yet three of the most famous Ashes ended in English wins: the BODYLINE controversy of 1932–33, Ian Botham's one-man show in 1981 and the near-miracle of 2005. All three are invariably referred to as 'proud chapters', which in turn are part of a 'rollercoaster narrative'. Never have a few grains of dust been elevated so far above their status.

See also ALL-ROUNDER; BRADMAN, SIR DONALD; FOLLOW-ON; STUMPS.

ASKING RATE

The rate required, in runs per over, by the team chasing a target. When Australia are fielding, the asking rate could easily be confused with the number of appeals per delivery.

See also HOWZAT.

AVERAGES

Just as FOOTBALLERS claim without the slightest trace of irony that they would rather have secured the three points than scored a HAT-TRICK, so cricketers will pretend they don't know their latest batting or bowling average. Five pints later, they will be quoting it to two decimal places and explaining exactly how many runs they need to score in the final innings of the season to claim moral superiority over their team-mates.

Let's not be coy about this in a 'statistics are for saddos' kind of way. Averages matter. In one sense, they are a bald, bland piece of maths: the product of dividing runs scored by number of times dismissed (for batsmen), or runs conceded by number of wickets taken (for bowlers). In another sense, they are a scarily public measure of a player's performance and, if you're a county cricketer, the route either to a new two-year contract or to the door marked 'EXIT'. Average over 40 with the bat or under 30 with the ball, and you'll have nothing to worry about. A good trick is to begin the season with a couple of cheap unbeaten hundreds against university sides in the hope that, come September, the committee has forgotten which team you scored them against. (You might laugh, but many a FIRST-CLASS career has been based on this tactic.)

The most famous Test average is Don BRADMAN's tantalizing 99.94, but it is not the highest. That honour goes to Andy Ganteaume, the Trinidadian wicketkeeper who became living proof of Disraeli's maxim about lies, damned lies and statistics when he made 112 for West Indies against England at Port-of-Spain in February 1948 in what turned out to be his only Test innings. But when the England selectors of the 1980s and '90s inadvertently mimicked their West Indian counterparts by repeatedly dropping players after one game, the tactic proved strangely ineffectual.

The explanation for the Ganteaume Conundrum is that he was almost certainly axed for scoring his century too slowly. As he approached three figures, Ganteaume and his batting partner, Frank Worrell, were handed a note written by their captain, Gerry Gomez. 'I want you to push on now,' it read. 'We are behind the clock and need to score more quickly.' While Worrell went on to become one of the most prolific batsmen of his generation and the first black captain of West Indies, Ganteaume never got the chance to redeem himself. Still, at least it meant he retired with a better average than Bradman.

See also INVINCIBLES; STONEWALL; TREADMILL; WS, THE THREE.

BAGGY GREEN

Some Australians like to think of the Baggy Green – the cap awarded to all Australian Test debutants – as possessing special powers. In fact, it is just a piece of cloth, but if you offer this view in a Sydney pub the punters will cover their ears and start wailing until you have shut up. Steve Waugh spoke of the Baggy Green's 'aura' and believed that if you fell asleep wearing it you would be able to see in the dark and walk through walls, which is why he wore the same one throughout his eighteen-year career. His patriotism was impressively unerring, but some felt he took things too far by wearing it to watch his fellow Aussie Pat Rafter in a tennis match at Wimbledon. Mike Atherton claimed it was 'enough to make you puke', which was harsh but fair, although he might secretly have wished that England's own cap inspired such pride. Then again, the Neatly Fitting Blue never sounded quite right.

Waugh was not the first Australian Test cricketer to wear his Baggy Green out of hours. Chuck Fleetwood-Smith, the CHINAMAN bowler whose final bowling analysis in Test cricket was 1 for 298 against England at The Oval during Len Hutton's match in 1938, once wore his to a drinking session on the banks of the Yarra in Melbourne, only for a swift 'tsk tsk' from a fellow boozer to dissuade him from repeating the crime. Bill Lawry wore his while cleaning out his pigeon loft, which was enough to convince his wife Joy that it belonged in the bin. At the far end of the disloyalty spectrum comes Ian Chappell, who was given about ten Baggy Greens over the course of his fifteen-year Test career and might have sparked demonstrations in the streets of Adelaide when he ventured the view that 'a cricket cap is a cap'. Still, the mythology lives on, and in 2003 the Baggy Green worn by Don BRADMAN during the 1948 tour of England was sold to an unnamed buyer by Ludgrove's auctioneers in Australia for a reputed $A425,000 (£172,000).

See also INVINCIBLES.

BALL

'Hey, Viv,' snarled the Glamorgan fast bowler Greg Thomas at Viv Richards after he had beaten his outside edge in a county match. 'It's round, it's red and it weighs five ounces.' Folklore has it that Richards, playing for Somerset, responded by hitting Thomas's next ball out of the ground. 'You know what it looks like, now you go and find it.'

If there had been enough time, Thomas would surely have pointed out to Richards that a cricket ball contains cork and latex rubber covered by twine. And that the four leather quarters which make up its shiny red casing (or white, if you are playing one-day cricket) are held together around the ball's circumference – which measures between 8 $\frac{13}{16}$ and 9 inches – by six pieces of string known as the SEAM. He might also have refined his ill-considered 'five ounces' jibe by pointing out that the ball must in fact weigh between 5 $\frac{1}{2}$ and 5 $\frac{3}{4}$ ounces. And, if Richards had continued to play and miss, Thomas's next blow would have been the revelation that the first modern ball – six seams and all – was manufactured in 1780 by Dukes of Penshurst in Kent.

He might even have wished that he had been bowling with a white ball, which seems to SWING more than its red cousin, possibly because of its hard, polyurethane coating which stops the ball getting dirty. Or he might simply have concluded that hurling a small red object at a man holding a piece of wood is generally a pretty thankless task.

See also FISHING; HELMETS; SLEDGING.

BALL-TAMPERING

Apparently it's always gone on, which is why the ex-pros yawn and look the other way whenever a bowler is caught contravening Law 42.3, governing 'The match ball – changing its condition'. But the authorities and non-ex-player journalists have been getting their knickers in a twist over ball-tampering ever since the start of the 1990s, when Pakistan's fast bowlers could barely draw breath without being accused of passing on their nefarious tips to the next generation of quicks.

In late 1990, the touring New Zealanders were so convinced that Pakistan had picked the SEAM during their victories in the first two Tests that Chris Pringle experimented with one or two tricks of his own during the third match at Faisalabad and ended up with 11 wickets for 152 (since the other 19 wickets he took in Tests came at an AVERAGE of 65, it's fair to say that Pringle's methods were effective).

Then, in 1992, Pakistan visited England and won the Test series 2–1 on the back of some astonishing spells with the old ball from Wasim Akram and Waqar Younis. England's batsmen cried foul, and when the umpires changed the ball during the fourth one-day international at LORD'S – but refused to explain why – the conspiracy theorists had heard all they needed. Allan Lamb was fined and suspended for outlining his grievances in the *Daily Mirror*, but the ICC swept the whole issue under the carpet. 'In the darkness,' wrote Scyld Berry in WISDEN, 'further seeds of mistrust and animosity were sown for the future.' Thirteen years later, when England reverse-swung their way to the ASHES, Wasim demanded an apology: while the Pakistanis had been called cheats for getting the ball to SWING violently and late, the English were held up as heroes.

The most common form of tampering is lifting the seam, which can create an air pocket and affect the way the ball moves in the air. But the application of what the Laws call an 'artificial substance' is just as old a trick. England's John Lever was rumoured to have used Vaseline to help him keep one side of the ball shiny on his way to figures of 7 for 46 in India's first innings at Delhi in 1976–77, and a match analysis of 10 for 70. Mike Atherton was caught on TV applying dirt from his pocket to the surface of the ball during the Lord's Test against South Africa in 1994, and faced calls for his resignation. And Imran Khan went even further and admitted years after the event that he had used a bottle top to gouge the ball during a county match for Sussex against Hampshire in 1981.

Occasionally, the culprit cannot be found. When Surrey were twice warned for lifting the quarter-seam – which runs perpendicular to the main seam – during a championship game against Nottinghamshire in 2005, a club investigation failed to unearth the villain, despite calls from inside the dressing-room to flush him out with a lie-detector test. Whispers that Surrey were all set to proceed until it was discovered that the lie-detector had been tampered with were unfounded.

See also ALL-ROUNDER; CUTLERY; MATCH-FIXING.

BARMY ARMY

Who are they? And where do they come from? These, it seems, are the questions on everyone's lips when they meet the Barmy Army, the rag-tag of solicitors, students, bank managers and blokes digging for oil in Kazakhstan who make up cricket's merriest band of supporters. The answer, chanted with inebriated pride, leaves little room for doubt: 'We are the England, the mighty, mighty England.' In the days when England's cricketers were far from mighty, the response could be laughed off as a spot of old-fashioned Anglo-Saxon self-deprecation. But while Michael Vaughan's team were winning six series in a row, culminating in the 2005 ASHES, it began to sound like a spot of old-fashioned Anglo-Saxon arrogance.

The Barmy Army emerged as a concept during England's tour of Australia in 1994–95, when the local media decided that anyone foolish enough to follow a rubbish cricket team around the world deserved something for their troubles. The noun 'army' generously conferred a sense of organization on the group, but that left them needing an adjective that rhymed. The options were few.

Since then, the Barmy Army has become synonymous with England's overseas series, often injecting mausoleum-like stadiums (see Christchurch, March 2002) with a dose of adrenalin. These days, English cricket's loyal foot soldiers have moved effortlessly into the world of commerce, selling official T-shirts on their official website to wear on their official tours. There are some who feel the Army has become infected with self-importance, and England's tour of Sri Lanka in 2003–04 saw the birth of a rival splinter group called the Wavy Navy. They sank without trace.

The old school, of course, regard the Barmies as insufferable oiks. 'These types, who are obviously sufficiently well-heeled to be able to afford Caribbean holidays, can be very hard to bear at home, too, especially when the "patriotism" gets out of hand,' sniffed the cricket historian Derek Birley. To which the Army might helpfully reply: 'Britons never never never shall be slaves.'

See also BEIGE BRIGADE; FANCY-DRESS.

BAT

In 1771 Thomas 'Shock' White turned up to a game in the Hampshire village of Hambledon – often referred to as the cradle of cricket – with a bat as wide as the stumps. His ruse, a bit like putting Giant Haystacks in goal, was all the more ingenious for being legal. Except that it wasn't legal for long. The Hambledon committee introduced emergency legislation limiting the width of the bat to 4¼ inches, and in 1835 the permissible length was decreed as 38 inches (the bat's weight is up to the batsman). Both measurements remain in force today, when the main concern for ICC match officials seems to be whether the various sponsors' logos are 3mm wider than they should be.

See also ALUMINIUM; WILLOW.

BEAMER

A beamer is a head-high FULL-TOSS, and rubs shoulders in sport's hall of shame with the RUGBY player who gouges his opponent's eye and the boxer who bolsters his glove with a horseshoe. Possibly because no one wants to countenance the alternative, a beamer is usually passed off as an accident. There is also a small yet significant school of thought which says it is nothing of the kind.

The temperamental West Indies fast bowler Roy Gilchrist once declared: 'I have searched the rule books, and there is not a word in any of them that says a fellow cannot bowl a fast full-toss at a batsman. A batsman has got a bat and they should get the treatment they deserve.' After liberally testing out his theory, Gilchrist was banished from the West Indian side and saw out his career in the Lancashire Leagues, where he attacked an Australian batsman with a stump during a charity match.

Rodney Hogg, an Australian paceman with a similarly aggressive outlook on life, is adamant that beamers – or bean-balls – are only ever deliberate. 'A bean-ball at the head is not a slip,' he insisted on Melbourne radio in 2005. 'It's a cold, calculated piece of the game. When you release a bean-ball, you are releasing it at a different part of your action. You have to release the ball earlier. I must confess I used to bowl a few bean-balls. It was part of the game. There was no rule that said you couldn't. I believed at the time, when some wickets were so flat and there was no bounce on them, I could even things up with a couple of bean-balls. You could hit blokes in the head in those days and after the game have a drink with them. These days, you could end up in court.'

The New Zealand coach John Bracewell hinted as much

when he suggested that Brett Lee's repeated use of the delivery against his team could lead to legal action. But by and large the game regulates itself. Waqar Younis was removed from the attack during the 2003 World Cup game between Pakistan and Australia after bowling two beamers at Andrew Symonds, who was on his way to a match-winning 143 not out. *WISDEN* noted gravely that Waqar 'apologized after the first, but showed no remorse for the second'. And when Lancashire's Wasim Akram hit Derbyshire's Chris Adams flush on the back during the final of the Benson & Hedges Cup in 1993, the two players later squared up in the LORD's pavilion, where any argument usually centres on who spilled the gin and tonic.

Just about the only universally popular beamer ever bowled came out of the hand of Inzamam-ul-Haq, who pinned George W. Bush during the American President's visit to Hyderabad in March 2006. Inzamam was supposed to be teaching Bush the basics of cricket, but instead showed him what it feels like to be on the receiving end of an unprovoked attack. Mercifully for Pakistan–US relations, Bush was hit with a tennis ball.

See also BALL-TAMPERING; CUTLERY; MATCH-FIXING; USA; YORKER.

BEIGE BRIGADE

New Zealand's answer to the BARMY ARMY, the Beige Brigade have the same unremittingly positive outlook on life, which is just as well given that most talented Kiwi sportsmen are pinched by RUGBY. They get their name from the gloriously tasteless kit worn by their national side in one-day games during the late 1970s and '80s, and achieved such notoriety that the coffee-and-mud colours were revisited during the first-ever men's TWENTY20 international between New Zealand and Australia at Auckland in February 2005. Catchphrase: 'It's about passion. Not fashion.'

BENAUD, RICHIE (1930–)

Rarely have two words meant so much to so many. For forty-two English summers, 'Morning, everyone' encapsulated Richie Benaud's contribution to cricket commentary: sparing, understated, yet somehow full of authority. Most viewers regarded him as the face of the sport, and a few even attended Test matches wearing oversized Richie masks; many regarded him as the voice of cricket too, and his nasal, Australian timbre has always proved too great a temptation to the Rory Bremner lurking in us all.

As the crowd rose to applaud his final commentary stint in England towards the end of the fifth ASHES Test at The Oval in September 2005 (he continued to commentate in Australia for Channel 9), it was easy to forget that he had once made a name for himself as one of the most adventurous ALL-ROUNDERS and captains in the history of the game. But for two generations of British viewers, Benaud was known as the kindly guide to one Test series after another. His trademark was the dry witticism, imparted with an almost audible flicker of the eyebrow and the gentlest of smirks. Once, when Jonty Rhodes was running England's fielders ragged during a Test at LORD'S, the summarizer, Chris Broad, groping for the word 'superlatives', admitted: 'You run out of expletives to describe this man.' After a moment's silence, Benaud wondered gently: 'Which particular one did you have in mind?'

Benaud's love of the pregnant pause might have won him the lead role in a play by Harold Pinter, a cricket nut himself, and there were those who wondered why he didn't use his unparalleled experience – it is thought that no one has been present at more Tests than he has – to express more trenchant opinions. Instead, viewers had to make do with his sporadic disgust at the front-foot no-ball law (don't ask). Splenetics were simply not his style.

On several occasions he has attempted to distil his broadcasting secrets into a few Benaudesque maxims. He told WISDEN: 'Put your brain into gear before opening your mouth. Never say "we" if referring to a team. Discipline is essential; fierce concentration is needed at all times.' Expressed like that, it all seemed so obvious really. But behind the apparently uncomplicated modus operandi – and the inevitable cream jacket – lay a tireless mind and an avaricious gatherer of cricketing news and gossip. He was usually one step ahead of the game, sometimes two.

Things were no different while he was captaining Australia to only four defeats in twenty-eight Tests between 1958 and 1963. He was a pugnacious lower-order batsman, an attacking leg-spinner (he remains a mentor to Shane Warne) and a hard-nosed leader unafraid to take a risk. At TEA on the last day of the epic Test against West Indies at Brisbane in December 1960, Australia were struggling at 109 for 6 in pursuit of 233. Benaud, one of the not-out batsmen, was asked by the chairman of selectors, Don BRADMAN: 'What's it going to be?' Knowing that Bradman had told the players before the start of the series that, in Benaud's words, 'The selectors would be looking in kindly fashion on players who played aggressively, who thought about the people paying their money at the turnstiles, who made the game attractive, and who won doing those things,' he replied: 'Well, we're going for a win.' 'I'm very pleased to hear it,' said Bradman. Benaud went out and extended his seventh-wicket stand with Alan Davidson to a virtually match-winning 134, before the last four Australian wickets fell for six runs to ensure Test cricket's first-ever TIE. Marvellous effort that, as Benaud might have put it.

See also CREASE; EXTRAS; FANCY-DRESS; GOOGLY; PACKER, KERRY.

BENEFIT

The benefit of the doubt traditionally goes to the batsman, so where does that leave doubts about the benefit? County cricket's benefit system is either criticized for being little more than legalized begging, or it is defended for rewarding longevity and loyalty. The premise is simple. If a player has represented a county for ten years or so, he will probably be granted a benefit season, in which he gets the chance to raise as much money as possible to help him through the melancholy years of his retirement.

Windfalls vary: Mike Atherton of Lancashire and Graeme Hick of Worcestershire collected over £300,000 each; Derbyshire's Allan Warner picked up just £19,000. Some players love being in the limelight; others dread the prospect of yet another cheese-and-wine evening or tie-auctioning bonanza. But thanks to a House of Lords decision in 1927 (*Reed* v *Seymour*), all proceeds are tax-free, a dreamy state of affairs that relies on a wink-and-nudge agreement between players and officials to not mention the prospect of a benefit in their contracts.

Critics point out that the system encourages older players to hang around for their golden handshake and block the paths of promising youngsters, although a domestic structure that supports eighteen FIRST-CLASS counties is hardly short of opportunities. Australians argue that it represents all that is wrong about the English game: geriatric fielders, money ahead of pride, and fund-raising barbecues that are hardly worthy of the name. The English respond by brandishing their tax-free cheques and buying a holiday home on Brisbane's Gold Coast.

See also TREADMILL.

BITS AND PIECES

Semi-pejorative term for an ALL-ROUNDER who bats a bit (usually around No. 7, unless a spot of PINCH-HITTING is required) and bowls a bit too (usually second or third change, and almost always at medium-pace). As John Arlott observed about the New Zealander Bob Cunis, bits-and-pieces cricketers are 'neither one thing nor the other'. Classics of the genre include David Capel, any number of New Zealanders, and virtually the entire England squad that won the Akai-Singer Champions Trophy in SHARJAH in December 1997. Bits-and-pieces players tend to be exposed in Test cricket, where hustle and bustle is not quite enough. But their depression is soon lifted when they score 15 not out from 12 balls and take 1 for 30 from 7 overs in a meaningless one-day fixture shortly afterwards, at which point they are hailed as 'salt of the earth'.

See also MILITARY MEDIUM; *TEST MATCH SPECIAL*.

BLOCKHOLE

To the batsman, the blockhole is the part of the CREASE where he taps his bat while the bowler runs in. To the bowler, it is the perfect place to aim the YORKER. Get six balls an over in the blockhole and the cricketing world is your oyster, particularly in the closing stages of a one-day innings when batsmen love to give themselves room to free their arms. Like a hungry boa constrictor, the block-hole delivery oozes claustrophobia.

BODYLINE

Depending on whether you prefer warm ale in a village pub, or freezing lager while tending to the barbie, Body-line was a masterfully executed plan by the English to tame Don BRADMAN, or a dastardly piece of cheating designed to assert the supremacy of the mother country. Or possibly both. Either way, England's decision to use their fast bowlers in the winter of 1932–33 to aim a barrage of leg-stump deliveries at the Australians' bodies worked a treat. Bradman AVERAGED 56 – a feast for anyone else, mere peanuts by his own exalted standards – and Douglas Jardine's side won the series 4–1. But the stats tend to be forgotten. This was the most acrimonious Test series in the history of the game, and not merely because Jardine's Harlequin cap – a deliberately provocative symbol of class-conscious England – wound the Aussies up something rotten.

Bodyline was the direct result of Bradman's run-glut in 1930, when he scored a mind-boggling 974 runs in seven innings to help Australia regain the urn they had lost eighteen months earlier. Jardine, who had honed his vowels at Winchester and Oxford, and regarded all

Australians as 'an uneducated and unruly mob', decided something – anything – had to be done. So he hatched a plan which involved bouncing the hell out of Bradman and Co. while a packed leg-side field waited like vultures for the ricochets. An Australian journalist christened the tactic 'Bodyline', but Jardine preferred 'Fast-Leg-Theory', which is a bit like referring to the guillotine as a neck massage.

Some smelled trouble in advance. On hearing that Jardine had been appointed captain for the tour, his old cricket coach at Winchester reportedly said: 'Well, we shall win the ASHES – but we may lose a dominion.' He was nearly right, and more than seventy years later most Australians still regard Bodyline as a crime second only to Jason Donovan's *Greatest Hits*. The English, meanwhile, take disproportionate pleasure in reversing the old stereotype and calling Australia's grumble the longest whinge in sporting history.

Jardine's chief enforcers were Harold Larwood and Bill Voce, two fast bowlers from Nottinghamshire. But not all the England players shared their captain's ruthlessness. Gubby Allen refused to bowl Bodyline, while the Nawab of Pataudi turned down his request to field in the leg-trap during the first Test at Sydney. 'I see his Highness is a conscientious objector,' sneered Jardine. Pataudi was dropped after the second game, having made a slow century in the first. Not even Indian royalty was going to get in the way.

Generally, though, the English were all too happy to play to orders, and – with Bradman absent owing to fatigue – duly won the first Test by ten wickets, despite Stan McCabe's swashbuckling 187 not out. Australia levelled the series at Melbourne, but it was not until the third Test in the normally tranquil surroundings of Adelaide that blood began to boil. In front of a packed house of over 50,000, Larwood hit the Australia captain, Bill Woodfull, over the heart, prompting Jardine to summon his leg-side fielders into action for the start of Larwood's next over. The crowd howled in anger; the Australian selector Bill Johnson called it 'the most unsportsmanlike act ever witnessed on an Australian cricket field'. Woodfull immediately had his bat knocked out of his hand, and wickets began to tumble.

Back in the dressing-room Woodfull was visited by the England manager Pelham Warner. 'There are two teams out there,' said the Australia captain in a line that might have been dreamed up for the film of the series made in 1984, 'but only one of them is playing cricket.' When Larwood hit the Australia wicketkeeper Bert Oldfield on the head two days later – again bowling to a conventional field – mounted police moved into position on the BOUNDARY. A riot was only narrowly averted.

England won the match, and the next two, but the wheels of diplomacy were already turning. The Australian Cricket Board sent a cable to the MCC back at LORD'S: 'Unless stopped at once [Bodyline] is likely to upset the friendly relations existing between Australia and England.' The MCC replied with the haughtiness of a Dickensian schoolmaster. 'We, Marylebone Cricket Club, deplore your cable.' (Translation: 'Get back in your box, you colonial maggots.') In an unashamed bout of imperial muscle-flexing, Jardine then refused to play on unless the Australians withdrew their accusation of unsportsmanlike behaviour. Fuming at the injustice of it all, yet all too aware of their political impotence, the Australians did precisely as they were told.

Things unravelled pretty quickly after that as the MCC,

fearful of further diplomatic kerfuffle, sought to distance themselves from the men who had brought home the Ashes. Jardine captained England only six more times, and in 1935 the MCC officially condemned the tactics and introduced a new law stating that no more than two men could field behind square on the leg-side. Larwood never played Test cricket again and, believing he had been scapegoated by the English establishment, emigrated to – where else? – Australia. Fifty years on, he was still getting hate-mail. And Australians – the same ones who would chant 'kill, kill' as a rampant Dennis Lillee ran in to bowl – were still moaning.

See also ALUMINIUM; BOUNCER.

BOUNCER

The fast-bowlers' party line is that the bouncer – a ball that threatens the batsman's skull not his stumps – is supposed to intimidate rather than injure. In private, nothing gives them greater pleasure than the nauseating crunch of leather on flesh. Throw in a broken bone or two, preferably the opposition captain's index finger, and they can tackle their evening meal of raw ox with even greater relish.

Bowlers love bouncers – or bumpers – for several reasons: they can cause pain, they quickly reveal any weaknesses in the batsman's mind or technique, and they help manoeuvre him around his CREASE. Often two bouncers will be followed by a YORKER, by which time the batsman's weight will have been transferred fatally onto the back foot. So there was outcry among the fast-bowlers' union when bouncers were limited in the early 1990s to one per over. 'It's a stupid rule,' seethed Pakistan's Wasim Akram. 'Everyone in county cricket thinks that it's only been brought in to protect one batsman, and that's Graeme Hick.' The thought might even have occurred to Hick himself.

These days, bowlers are allowed to bowl two bouncers an over in Test cricket, and one an over in one-day internationals. But Hick was not the only player to be exposed by the short ball. Michael Bevan was probably the best one-day batsman in the history of the game, but he AVERAGED only 29 in eighteen Tests for Australia because bowlers soon worked out that, to use the technical term, he didn't 'like it up him'.

Paradoxically, some bowlers have used bouncers to induce a false sense of security. In the words of Ian Botham, the Antiguan Andy Roberts, who took 202 wickets in forty-seven Tests for West Indies, was 'the only one who's ever attempted dental surgery on me without a local anaesthetic, drill or any recognized tools of the trade'. Botham was playing in a one-day game for Somerset against Hampshire in 1974 when he foolishly HOOKED a Roberts bouncer for six. Unbeknown to the eighteen-year-old Botham, the Roberts bouncer came in two flavours: fast and speed of light. Guess which came next. Botham thought about the hook, then decided to protect his unhelmeted head with his glove. 'In the event, the impact of the ball smacking into my glove forced my own fist into my jaw, knocking out one tooth on the left-hand side and shattering two others clean in half on the right.' But men were men back then, and Botham hung around to score the winning runs before spending the next day undergoing dentistry of a more conventional kind.

Other bouncers have been life-threatening or worse.

On his debut for New Zealand at Auckland in February 1975, Ewen Chatfield's life was saved only by swift action from the England physio, Bernard Thomas, after his heart stopped beating following a blow on the left temple from Peter Lever. India's Nari Contractor had to undergo several operations after ducking into a delivery from Charlie Griffith in a game against Barbados in 1962–63. And during a match at LORD'S against MCC in 1870, the Nottinghamshire batsman George Summers was hit on the head by Jack Platts, who was making his first-class debut. Summers died a few days later, while Platts eventually took up slow bowling.

Except in the most serious instances, bowlers tend to affect little concern for the batsman they have just sconed. But Andre Nel has never done things by the rules. Nel was once offered 1,000 rand by his provincial coach, Ray Jennings, if he hit his childhood idol Allan Donald on the head in a domestic game in South Africa. Nel obliged, but promptly burst into tears when Donald collapsed in a heap. Jennings was furious. 'His hero ducks into a short one so what does he do?' he said, displaying all the compassion and sensitivity which he later showered on the South African national side. 'He goes and sobs over him like a girl guide.' Nel's home-help badge followed shortly after.

See also FLAT-TRACK BULLY; HELMETS; LONG-HOP.

BOUNDARY

The edge of the playing area, usually denoted by a rope (by which several English fielders have wanted to hang themselves following a blunder in front of a baying Melbourne mob). Also, the generic term for fours and sixes, even if it is often wrongly used to pertain exclusively to fours. Players who are transformed into foaming-at-the-mouth hooligans when they cross the boundary are said to suffer from white-line fever. This phenomenon usually refers to cricketers who *enter* the field of play rather than leave it, but if you know of any examples of the latter, be sure to notify the police.

BOX

One of the least visible but most important parts of a batsman's – and wicketkeeper's – equipment. An unwritten but widely observed rule states that whenever anyone is hit in the region commonly known as 'amidships', the fielding side, the two umpires and even the man batting at the other end (yes, his own team-mate and supposed ally) will immediately try – and fail – to stifle their laughter. The TV commentators will then announce, through barely suppressed guffaws, that 'for some reason, everyone always finds that very amusing. Except for the batsman!'

Occasionally, not even the box – or 'abdominal protector' as sufferers of verbal diarrhoea know it – can stand up to the battering. When England toured Australia in 1974–75, the future England coach David Lloyd was hit so forcefully in the groin by the Pom-hating tearaway Jeff Thomson that he had to be helped from the field, where he discovered that his box had been turned inside out. The injury, he noted later, confirmed 'my earlier statement about "Thommo" that I could play him with my cock, though some in the team thought it to be an extreme way of proving the point'. In a variation on a theme, the World Cup-winning former captain of the England WOMEN's team, Rachael Heyhoe-Flint, used to refer to her box as 'my manhole cover'. Less graphically, the box is also the old name given to the fielder in the gully, and is the shortened form of 'press box', where the media explain how it really should have been done out there.

See also FIELDING POSITIONS; ICC.

BRADMAN, SIR DONALD (1908–2001)

To describe Don Bradman as a useful batsman is like saying Shakespeare knew how to cobble together a sentence or Michelangelo was handy with a chisel. He was born to score runs, and then score some more. His Test AVERAGE of 99.94 – as integral a part of Australian culture as Uluru, Ned Kelly, and Dame Edna Everage – made him more than half as good again as his nearest rival. In 1949 he became the first sportsman to be knighted before he had retired. And when WISDEN named its Five Cricketers of the Century in 2000, Bradman uniquely received a nomination from each member of the 100-strong panel. Rumours that GOD was keeping a seat warm for him at his right-hand side remain unsubstantiated.

But perhaps the greatest compliment it is possible to pay him came from Nelson Mandela after he emerged from his Cape Town prison in 1990 following twenty-seven years of incarceration. Quite simply, he wanted to know whether Bradman was still alive. He should have known better: Bradman, eighty-one at the time, rarely made less than 90. When he died at the age of ninety-two, the only surprise was that, having never fallen in the nineties during his Test career, he had now done so in real life.

The English, who had Hobbs and Hammond but no

Bradman, can still guarantee a rise out of Australians by dismissing the Don as a soulless machine. 'So is a majestically flying aeroplane,' retorted the cricket writer Neville Cardus, who was lucky enough to see him bat. And Bradman certainly soared to heights others could only imagine. During Australia's 1930 tour of England, he manufactured scores of 131 at Trent Bridge, 254 at LORD'S (his favourite innings), 334 at Headingley and 232 at The Oval. His appeal was so great that summer that when Dai Davies almost bowled him during the game against Glamorgan, he was immediately removed from the attack: Glamorgan wanted to keep Bradman at the CREASE for Bank Holiday Monday to maximize gate receipts. His feats were enough to inspire England's controversial BODYLINE tactics for the return series in 1932–33, possibly the only time in Test history that an entire methodology has been devised to deal with one man.

'Stripped to the truth, he was a solitary man with a solitary aim,' wrote R. C. Robertson-Glasgow. But try telling that to cash-strapped Australians during the Depression of the 1920s and '30s. To them, he was nothing less than a deity. So what was the secret of his success? His former team-mate Jack Fingleton believed it was mental as much as physical. 'His mind gave his body no rest,' he wrote in *Brightly Fades the Don*. 'His mind called the tune and his body, gifted as it was in peerless footwork, eyesight, judgment and a perfect dynamo of ceaseless energy, danced to it. The only times the dance became agitated were against Bodyline and on STICKY pitches.'

Bradman did not disappoint until the very end. Needing four runs in his final Test innings at The Oval in 1948 to finish with a batting average of exactly 100, he was bowled second ball for nought by an Eric Hollies GOOGLY.

Commentating for BBC radio at the time, John Arlott wondered whether Bradman had been rendered misty-eyed by the England fielders' three cheers as he walked out to bat. Jack Crapp, standing at first slip, said later: 'That bugger Bradman never had a tear in his eye throughout his whole life,' which might have been closer to the truth. Still, at least England had denied him a three-figure Test average. As consolations go, it was like finding 10p after throwing away a winning lottery ticket.

See also FIELDING POSITIONS; INVINCIBLES; JOURNALISM; MASTER, THE.

BUFFET

Buffet – or cafeteria – bowling is bowling of such a poor standard that the batsmen simply help themselves. Buffet bowlers tend to serve up a delectable assortment of FULL-TOSSES, HALF-VOLLEYS and LONG-HOPS, and batsmen are well aware that it would be rude to say no.

BUMP BALL

In mechanical terms, a bump ball is a ball which is hit firmly into the ground before flying into the air and often tricking spectators into thinking a catch has been taken. In socio-cricketing terms, it might well have been the start of the widely accepted modern practice of batsmen waiting for the umpire's decision.

On the opening morning of the first post-war ASHES series at Brisbane, Don BRADMAN had scratched his way to 28 after Australia had lost two early wickets. Then it happened. The left-arm seamer Bill Voce, a BODYLINE veteran, sent down a full-length delivery which Bradman tried to chop through the CORDON. Instead, the ball flew straight to second slip, where Jack Ikin took a smart chest-high catch. The batsman, though, stayed put, thinking – or perhaps hoping – that it had been a bump ball. The umpires agreed, and Bradman went on to make 187 and set up an innings win for Australia. At the end of the over, England's captain, Wally Hammond, convinced the catch had been legitimate, is supposed to have snarled at Bradman: 'That's a fine fucking way to start the series.' Ah, the good old days.

In his biography of Bradman, Charles Williams writes: 'At least one captain of England takes the view that the practice of waiting for the umpire's decision even when there is no doubt and, indeed, of protesting against the umpire's decision, became the fashion that it is today not least because of what occurred in Brisbane on 29 November 1946.'

England have also been involved in more recent examples of controversial bump balls. Shivnarine Chanderpaul was caught behind off Angus Fraser at Bridgetown in March 1998 when replays showed that the ball had bounced before it reached Alec Stewart's gloves. Dominic Lawson, then editor of the *Sunday Telegraph*, later asked one of England's slip fielders whether he knew Chanderpaul had been diddled. 'Yes,' he said. 'It was fairly obvious.'

At Kandy in March 2001, England were equally unapologetic. Sri Lanka's Sanath Jayasuriya CUT Andy Caddick hard into the ground, only for Graham Thorpe to fly like a bird at third slip and pull off a sensational catch. Perhaps overwhelmed by Thorpe's athleticism, the umpire gave Jayasuriya out, which prompted the batsman to hurl his HELMET towards the pavilion while being goaded by a disgraceful bunch of red-faced England supporters. Mike Atherton named that series as the most acrimonious he had ever played in. Jayasuriya had another name for it.

See also FIELDING POSITIONS; SLEDGING; WALKING.

BUMPER

Another name for a BOUNCER (of the short-pitched-ball variety, rather than the shaven-headed-former-convict-scaring-punters-at-pubs variety).

BUNSEN

Rhyming slang is not really cricket's thing, but this one is an exception. A turning pitch – one that helps the spinners – is also known as a bunsen, for the obvious reason that Bunsen burner rhymes with turner. It is a phrase you tend to hear only from slow bowlers from the south-east of England, and mainly from Phil Tufnell. Upon sighting a bunsen, the likes of Tufnell can be expected to rub their hands together gleefully and exclaim 'Lovely jubbly.'

See also CHARACTER; MICHELLE; TURN.

CALYPSO CRICKET

It all started in 1950 when Sonny Ramadhin and Alf Valentine took 18 wickets to spin West Indies to their first Test win at LORD'S, prompting the Trinidadian songsters Lord Kitchener (not that one) and Lord Beginner to pen a celebratory calypso. It began with the line 'Cricket, lovely cricket', and finished with 'those two little pals of mine / Ramadhin and Valentine'. Thereafter, any expression of West Indian exuberance would be referred to as calypso cricket. As long as West Indies kept winning, which they did almost without fail between 1980 and 1994, the phrase connoted joyful liberation and expression. But when things began to go wrong in the mid-1990s, it conveyed nothing more than amateurishness. Calypso cricket became calypso collapso as West Indies lost one Test after another. The songs, not surprisingly, have dried up.

See also: CHUCKING; INITIALS; REARGUARD.

CARRY YOUR BAT

A much-abused phrase, mainly because it is often applied to any batsman who is not out at the end of a side's completed innings. This is not so: only openers who are still undefeated when their team is all out can properly be said to have carried their bats, and it does not happen very often. The 2006 WISDEN lists forty-one instances in Test cricket, three of them – a record – by the West Indian Desmond Haynes, who was also last out in both innings in the first Test against New Zealand at Dunedin in February 1980.

Glenn Turner's 223 out of 386 for New Zealand against West Indies at Kingston in February 1972 was the highest score on the list, but special mention must be made of Geoff Boycott, who was the only Test player to have carried his bat for 99. 'I could have strangled Bob Willis,' he remarked years after England's No. 11 had fallen for a DUCK to Australia's Geoff Dymock at Perth in December 1979, with Boycott stranded one short of another milestone. Whether the feeling was mutual can only be guessed at.

The lowest score was 26, by Bernard Tancred for South Africa against England at Cape Town in March 1889. If that sounds pretty feeble, then he was left with little option. The next-best effort in the innings was William Milton's 7 as South Africa replied to England's 292 with a total of 47. FOLLOWING ON, they were bowled out for 43 as the slow left-armer Johnny Briggs returned the ridiculous match figures of 15 for 28. And they say cricket isn't what it used to be.

But, according to Bill Frindall, the lowest score in all FIRST-CLASS cricket by a bat-carrier is 5, by Dick Barlow for Lancashire against Nottinghamshire at Trent Bridge in 1882. Barlow, who made his runs out of a puny Lancashire total of 69 on a RAIN-affected pitch, was known for his defensive qualities, which makes you wonder about the following lines in Francis Thompson's nostalgic poem 'At LORD'S': 'As the run-stealers flicker to and fro / To and fro / O my Hornby and my Barlow long ago.' Presumably most of the stealing was done by Hornby.

See also RABBIT; REARGUARD; STONEWALL.

CEEFAX

Only the true cricket fan can appreciate the thrill of staring at a screen full of numbers that change every minute or so, and even then do not really change very much. It might be less fast-moving than the Stock Exchange, but it is far more interesting and – ignore what the City boys in their fancy striped jackets say – a lot more stressful. Before the internet changed everything, Ceefax (page 340, as if you didn't know) used to be the most reliable way of following the progress of your county team. Long pauses between updates were usually bad news: it meant the person inputting the data was struggling to spell 'lbw b Kasprowicz'. But generally, Ceefax was reassuring: statistically speaking, after all, a wicket was unlikely to fall next ball, was it? So if I just keep the TV on all day . . .

Ceefax was also the place where cricketers would learn they had been picked for the 1989 ASHES series. These days, the England management makes a point of phoning new selections before the happy news becomes public. Back in 1989, when twenty-nine different players contributed to a 4–0 mauling at the hands of Australia, it was tempting to imagine there might not have been the time, money or manpower to ring them all. 'My friend's just seen my name on Ceefax, and I'm over the moon,' was the common response of many a starry-eyed English youngster who would never be heard of again after scoring a pair on his Test debut.

See also CRICINFO; DUCK.

CHARACTER

To possess 'character' is a mixed blessing. On one hand, it means you have grit, gumption and bottle. On the other, it can be a roundabout way of saying you're not very talented. But although cricketers with character are rarely the most gifted members of the side, they are among the most treasured. They are the ones who say things like 'There's no "I" in team' and genuinely mean it; who will spend an hour providing throwdowns for their more brilliant colleagues and get nothing in return; and who will happily volunteer for NIGHTWATCHMAN duties against Brett Lee. Coaches will tell you that a less able batsman with plenty of character has more potential than a highly skilled show-off with no character at all. But we all know which we'd rather be.

To be called 'a character' is a different matter altogether. Admission to this dubious group often requires little more than the ability to grow a silly moustache (Merv Hughes) or say 'Happy days' (Phil Tufnell) or swear a lot (Merv Hughes and Phil Tufnell). Characters rarely become characters before they have retired, at which point everyone begins to reminisce about the good old days, when the game was full of them.

Yes, we all want to have our cake and eat it (unless Hughes has got there first). In this highly professional era, we moan if our cricketers are too one-dimensional, then we moan if their foibles and peccadilloes prevent them from winning Test matches for England.

The ideal cricketer, then, is a character *with* character, which leaves you with Keith Miller, Ian Botham and Shane Warne. Still there's always nightwatchman duty . . .

See also ALL-ROUNDER; DRUGS; PRESSURE; SLEDGING; WONDERBALL.

CHIN MUSIC

In the more socially frivolous sections of 1920s America, chin music meant idle gossip. But the West Indies pace attacks of the 1980s did not regard it as a means of passing the time of day. As in baseball, chin music describes a delivery which passes so close to the batsman's head that he can practically smell the leather, hence its alternative description as a perfume ball. The music he might hear is more likely to be Chopin's *Funeral March* than 'The Birdie Song'.

See also BOUNCER; BUMPER.

CHINAMAN

The story goes that when the West Indies' left-arm spinner Ellis 'Puss' Achong, a Trinidadian of Chinese ancestry, had England's Walter Robins stumped at Old Trafford in 1933, Robins sloped off past umpire Joe Hardstaff Snr and grumbled: 'Fancy being done by a bloody Chinaman.' Standing nearby, the West Indian fielder Learie Constantine wondered: 'Do you mean the bowler or the ball?'

This is the most likely derivation of the Chinaman, the left-arm spinner's mirror-image of the right-armer's LEG-BREAK, which turns, in other words, from off-stump to leg (as opposed to the Chinaman GOOGLY, which is bowled out of the back of the left hand, turns from leg to off, and can inflict a serious headache on anyone grappling for the first time with the game's terminology). Achong was in fact a conventional slow left-armer, but his other delivery – the one which foxed Robins – was the ball that made him famous.

To confuse the issue, there are a few stubborn souls east of the Pennines – the sort who believe GOD grew up in Knaresborough – who have claimed the Chinaman as their own. When Maurice Leyland died in 1967, his county captain, David Burton, wrote: 'It was always thought in Yorkshire that the ball called "The Chinaman" originated from Maurice. A left-arm bowler, he sometimes bowled an enormous OFF-BREAK from round the wicket which, if not accurately pitched, was easy to see and to get away on the leg-side. In later days, laughing about this, he would say it was a type of ball that might be good enough to get the Chinese out if no one else. Hence this ball became Maurice's "Chinaman".'

Since Leyland's playing career lasted from 1920 until 1947, it is unclear whether his joke predates the Robins grumble. Whatever the etymology – and with apologies to Leyland's home town of Harrogate – the romance belongs fairly and squarely to Achong. Born in Trinidad in 1904 he had a (mainly) Chinese father and an Afro-Caribbean mother, which explains why the Chinese delegation that supposedly turned up to greet him as the touring West Indians arrived at Waterloo station in 1933 left disappointed. According to Scyld Berry, they had been expecting 'the full Mandarin'.

One newspaper report from that tour noted, in terms which would prick the racially attuned ears of today, that Achong 'varies his flight, break and pace as one of his imperturbable and intelligent race might be expected to do'. Even so, he played in only six Tests, all against England, and took just 8 wickets at 47 each. But he remains the only player of Chinese origin to have won a Test cap, and one of only two men – along with Bernard Bosanquet of Bosie fame – to have had a delivery named after him.

Among Achong's chief successors were the Yorkshireman Johnny Wardle, the Australians Jack Walsh and George Tribe, and even Garry Sobers. In the modern era, South Africa's Paul Adams employed such a bewildering action to send down his Chinamen and left-arm googlies that one journalist said he looked like a 'frog in a blender'. It remains the most imaginative phrase ever to have been reduced by overuse to a cliché.

See also ALL-ROUNDER; DISMISSALS; JOURNALISM.

CHINESE CUT

Also known as the French CUT, the Harrow cut and the Surrey drive, this is less exotic than it sounds. The Chinese cut describes a thick inside edge that whistles just past the stumps and usually away to fine leg for four. It is always fortuitous and invariably causes the bowler to question the batsman's biological provenance. Best accompanied by ironic descriptions like 'lovely' and 'well placed'.

See also SLEDGING.

CHOCOLATE CAKE

The preferred dessert of members of BBC radio's *TEST MATCH SPECIAL* commentary team, usually sent in by listeners. Brian Johnston used to be the main recipient, which would draw wry comments from the more earnest John Arlott. In Arlott's biography, David Rayvern Allen quotes a typical piece of his commentary, as remembered by the *TMS* scorer Bill Frindall. '[Brian] was a little upset on

Friday,' he would tell the listeners, 'because he didn't get anything, which means that a lot of you are actually eating your own food . . . Mrs Matthews of Penge, I'm afraid he doesn't think much of your nut brittle, because that's been discarded by the microphone . . .'

CHUCKING

Calling a bowler a chucker is like calling the tax man a fraudster, or Jeff Thomson a Pom. It is the slur of slurs, and careers have ended because of it. Along with MATCH-FIXING, BALL-TAMPERING and cheering in the press box, chucking is one of cricket's greatest no-nos, but that hasn't stopped it rearing its crooked arm every now and then. The Great Chucking Debate has been particularly ferocious on three occasions: at the turn of the twentieth century, in the late 1950s and early '60s, and today.

Australia's Ernie Jones became the first bowler to be no-balled for throwing in a Test, against England at Melbourne in January 1898. Not long after, C. B. Fry – otherwise regarded as a paragon of Victorian sporting virtue – decided that bowling was not for him after he was called four times. But it was not until after the war that chucking really began to threaten what some regarded as the very fabric of the game. Suddenly, you could barely move without walking head-first into a bent elbow. Paranoia grew rampant. It was, wrote David Frith, 'cricket's McCarthyite period'.

England's left-arm spinner Tony Lock, the man who took the other wicket when Jim Laker picked up 19 for 90 against Australia at Old Trafford in July 1956, remodelled his action after watching footage of himself bowling against New Zealand. South Africa's Geoff Griffin never

A textbook chuck

played another Test after being no-balled eleven times against England at LORD's in June 1960, but nobly refused to take the matter to court because he 'loved cricket too much to sully the great game further'. And there can be few more poignant photographs in sport than the one of Australia's Ian Meckiff standing in the outfield, head bowed, after Col Egar called him four times during the first Test against South Africa at Brisbane in December 1963. Despite winning his eighteenth cap in that game, Meckiff was dropped for good. Sonny Ramadhin of West Indies was smarter: he escaped censure only by bowling his assortment of spinners with sleeves buttoned down to the wrists.

Since the 1990s, most interest has focused on Sri Lanka's Muttiah Muralitharan, whose freakishly rubbery WRIST and congenital elbow condition – he is unable to straighten it fully – have kept the chucking police in a state of frenzied alert. The Australian umpire Darrell Hair no-balled him seven times at Melbourne in December 1995, before Ross Emerson called him during a one-day international against England at Adelaide in January 1999, despite the fact that Murali's action had already been cleared by the ICC. That match descended into acrimony as the Sri Lanka captain, Arjuna Ranatunga, threatened to take his whole team off the field, but the controversy rumbled on.

Many observers – mainly from the white Test nations – were convinced Murali was a chucker. Just as many – mainly Asians – disagreed. Insults flew and conspiracy theories were exchanged. The accusation of racism never felt more than another bent limb away. The ICC introduced permissible degrees of flexion in a bowler's elbow: 10 for fast bowlers, 7.5 for medium-pacers, 5 for spinners.

When Murali's DOOSRA was measured at 14 degrees, his accusers pretended to feel sorry for him. But the system seemed arbitrary, and in 2005 the ICC introduced a blanket figure of 15 degrees for all bowlers – the level at which a bowling action looks suspicious to the naked eye. In an atmosphere of name-calling and prejudice, this was pure common sense.

For Murali, though, the hounding did not stop. Australian crowds would greet his every delivery with a tedious cry of 'No-ball', and Murali pulled out of Sri Lanka's trip there in 2004 when the Prime Minister, John Howard, added his voice to that of the baying mob. After trying to prove his innocence by bowling with his arm in a splint for an experiment arranged by Channel 4 in 2004, Murali decided enough was enough during the VB Series in Australia in the early part of 2006, when one idiot in the crowd at Perth painted his face black and scrawled 'No-ball' across his chest. He voluntarily underwent yet another set of tests, which measured both his doosra and his OFF-BREAK at less than 13 degrees. And if that didn't silence his tormentors, the fact that other bowlers – such as England's James Kirtley, Pakistan's Shabbir Ahmed and South Africa's Johan Botha – had been banned in the meantime should have kept them happy.

See also ALBANIA; CALYPSO CRICKET; EXTRAS; UNDERARM BOWLING.

COFFIN

The morbid name given to the unfeasibly big trunks in which cricketers keep their kit, bats and porn mags. Delve into another player's coffin at your peril: dressing-rooms dislike rummagers, so it could prove to be the final nail in your own. Monty Bowden, who at 23 years and 144 days remains the youngest player to have captained England when he led them in the second of two Tests in South Africa in March 1889, was buried a couple of years later at the age of twenty-six in a coffin made out of whiskey cases. No, this was not some kind of sick ritual reserved for new captains: Bowden was in fact dead, having being trampled on by his own oxen after staying in Africa to set up a stockbroking business with Charles Aubrey Smith, England's captain in the first Test. But the animal kingdom was not finished yet. As Bowden's body awaited interment at the Umtali Hospital in what was then Rhodesia, it had to be protected from prowling lions.

See also FLANNELS.

COLLINS, A. E. J. (1885–1914)

He never played FIRST-CLASS cricket and was killed in action at Ypres aged twenty-nine, but Arthur Edward Jeune Collins is forever guaranteed a place in *WISDEN*. In 1899, at the age of thirteen, Collins hit an unbeaten 628 ('plus or minus 20 shall we say', according to one of the scorers) in a house match at Clifton College in Bristol. It is thought to be the highest score made in any form of organized cricket (no, the beach doesn't count), and – like Kevin Pietersen's self-confidence – is unlikely ever to be surpassed. Dropped on 50, 100, 140, 556, 605 and 619 (by which time the bowlers must have regarded cricket in the same way as Douglas Jardine regarded Australians), Collins helped Clarke's House to 836 over a period of four afternoons, hitting 1 six, 4 fives, 31 fours, 33 threes, 146 twos and 87 singles (boundaries earned only two, while anything hit down the slope had to be run). Just in case his peers didn't hate him enough already, Collins then took 11 wickets to dismiss North House for 87 and 61. Clarke's scraped home by an innings and 688. A career in the army got in the way of cricket, but, when you've made an undefeated sextuple-century, it's unlikely that a solid 36 for Gloucestershire against Glamorgan would have quite hit the mark.

See also BODYLINE; FRENCH CRICKET.

CORDON

The area between the wicketkeeper and the gully that is supposed to be on the patrol for thick edges and loose wafts. Traditionally, cordons at cricket matches have been manned by men in white, but these days shaven-headed heavies wearing fluorescent orange jackets and pretending to say important things into walkie-talkies have muscled in on the act by forming their own cordons around the BOUNDARY moments before the end of the game. Their aim is to prevent fans running on to the pitch; the effect is more like a blurred red rag to several alcohol-fuelled bulls. For some, the sight of three stewards crash-tackling a deliriously drunk New Zealander on the Oval outfield is worth the admission price alone. The Kiwi might later be cordoned off for the night in his very own cell in Wandsworth prison.

See also FIELDING POSITIONS; STREAKERS.

CORRIDOR OF UNCERTAINTY

It is tempting to imagine that this was the name given to the area outside Andrew Flintoff's hotel room following his post-ASHES all-nighter in 2005. But it would also be wrong. The 'corridor of uncertainty' is a phrase used to describe the area on and around off-stump which leaves batsmen unsure whether to play or leave. The best SEAM bowlers spend most of their careers lurking with intent in the corridor – and being praised by Geoffrey Boycott for doing so. 'The area I like to call the corridor of uncertainty' is Boycott's third-favourite way of starting a sentence, behind 'I' and 'Roobish'.

COVER-DRIVE

The crown prince of batting strokes, the cover-drive exists on a higher moral plane than the common-or-garden PULL shot or the two-a-penny square-CUT. It denotes good breeding, partly because it requires technique as well as timing, partly because it is played on the off-side, which is regarded as the hemisphere of the artist (the leg-side is the grubby realm of the artisan).

This is, of course, a load of garbage. A cover-drive for four is as valuable as a HOOK for four, and not quite as exhilarating. Its reputation as the apple of the coach's eye probably derives from the widespread conceit that batting is the nobler of cricket's two main arts – bowlers serve up, batsmen pick and choose – and that the stroke itself bespeaks effortlessness.

For this reason, the cover-drive is frequently prefaced with adjectives like 'silky', 'elegant', 'sumptuous' and 'exquisite'. If the batsman is left-handed, the aesthetics are for some reason amplified. Take David Gower. A generation of sports fans – or at least those unfortunate enough to have watched the BBC TV sports quiz *They Think It's All Over* on a regular basis – will have grown up believing that Gower's only shot was the nibble to first slip. In fact, he possessed the dreamiest cover-drive of them all.

See also FIELDING POSITIONS.

CREASE

There are three types of crease in cricket, unless you count the one on your FLANNELS which the village team's self-appointed old curmudgeon reckons you should be able to sharpen your pencil on (note to curmudgeon: very few people use pencils any more).

1. The popping crease is the line parallel to and 4 feet away from the stumps at both ends. It is where the batsman taps his bat when he is waiting for the ball to be delivered, unless he is Matthew Hayden, in which case the popping crease is a cruel yoke of oppression, and thus becomes a line 4 feet behind him. In theory, it runs the full width of the playing surface. The popping crease is so called because, to avoid being run out, batsmen used to have to place their bat in a small hole on the line before the ball was popped into it by a member of the fielding side. Just as batsmen must ground part of their bat behind the popping-crease to avoid being stumped or run out, so bowlers must land part of their foot behind it to avoid being no-balled. Frequent no-balls might persuade the fielding captain to pour sawdust over

the popping crease, ostensibly to prevent the bowler's front foot from slipping, but probably to obscure the umpire's view of the line itself, especially if the sawdust gets in his eye.

2. The bowling crease is the line, measuring 8ft 8in, on which the stumps stand. The standard length of a cricket pitch – 22 yards – is the distance between the two bowling creases. Since 1967 the no-ball law has pertained to the front foot, but until then the umpire had to check that part of the bowler's *back* foot landed behind the bowling crease. This resulted in neck ache for the umpires and inevitable rule-bending by the bowlers, who would drag their back foot as far forward as possible once they had delivered the ball.

3. The return crease is drawn perpendicular to the other two creases and joins up the popping and bowling creases at both ends of the pitch and on both sides of the stumps. In other words, it is 4ft 4in either side of middle stump, but you will be forgiven for not really caring any more. A no-ball will be called if the bowler's back foot crosses the return crease – a rare occurrence since the umpire is by now paranoid about missing the far more common front-foot no-ball.

See also BENAUD, RICHIE; DISMISSALS; EXTRAS.

CRICINFO

The home of cricket on the internet began life in 1993 when Dr Simon King, a British cricket-loving academic who had moved to the USA, decided to deal with his homesickness by setting up a website to deal with every fan's favourite question: 'What's the score?'

Cricinfo worked on a voluntary basis at first, but it soon became big business as people realized that the average cricket fan feeds off statistics like pandas devour bamboo. The site merged with *WISDEN* Online in February 2003, and in early 2006 was employing seventy staff, mainly in Mumbai and London. When Sachin Tendulkar hit an undefeated 95 to help India beat Pakistan in the third one-day international at Lahore on 13 February 2006, more than two million users logged on during the day for the first time. Only the official sites of baseball, basketball, and American football in the States attract more hits among single-sport websites.

CROSS-POLLINATION

Pre-match PRESS CONFERENCES rarely contain more than a few earnest promises to give 110 per cent (like inflation, the figure sneaks up every year) and to take every innings as it comes (how else?). So you can imagine the excited flurry of scribbles on notepads when the New Zealand captain, Stephen Fleming, began to bandy about heartfelt references to 'cross-pollination'. Cleverly adapting the language of the natural world, Fleming – who had been enjoying the autobiography of the former coach of Australia's RUGBY union side, Rod Macqueen – promised to enhance his own side's performance by borrowing techniques from other sports.

Would he be instructing his players to jostle the umpire after a dubious decision? Or to trap a member of the opposition in a half-nelson? Or to perform the haka at the start of every over? No, Fleming intended to sharpen up the New Zealanders' prowess in the field by sending them to watch major-league baseball matches in the USA. Although some critics were concerned the players would return with a worryingly intimate understanding of the skills involved in transporting five jumbo-sized cartons of popcorn along a row of obese Americans, Fleming's plan was not as wacky as it sounds. And it was soon put into action. When Brian Lara was run out during the World Cup game against West Indies at Port Elizabeth in February 2003, it was courtesy of a baseball-style relay throw from Lou Vincent at deep midwicket to Chris Cairns, who pulled off a direct hit at the non-striker's end from just outside the 30m fielding circle as Lara tried to get back for the third. CRICINFO's live ball-by-ball commentary records that the New Zealanders were 'beside themselves with excitement'.

Three years later New Zealand hired the services of Mike Young, a well-respected baseball coach, who had already worked with Australia and England. Beyond baseball, and to the consternation of the old school, county cricketers can regularly be seen warming up for yet another day's play with a game of FOOTBALL or touch rugby. 'How's that going to help their forward defensive?' has become one of the most frequently asked questions of the new millennium.

CUT

In cricket, as in life, cuts can be unkind. But they are more usually square, late, or upper, and very occasionally French or CHINESE. Square-cuts whistle through point off a horizontal bat, and reached their apotheosis in the form of Robin Smith during the 1989 ASHES. Uppercuts fly over the slips and dangerously close to third man. And late-cuts, which require such finesse that the bat momentarily resembles a wand, are caressed behind point and often greeted with cries of 'Ah, you don't see many of them any more!' The frequency of the observation suggests otherwise. French and Chinese cuts are the ugly ducklings of the flock, and impossible to practise. Cut can also describe the movement of the ball off the pitch. If spinners TURN it, then seamers cut it by rolling their fingers across the SEAM at the point of release. If the attempt goes wrong then 'cut' is very nearly what they might call themselves as the ball disappears for four.

See also FIELDING POSITIONS.

CUT STRIP

The pitch, chosen from several alternatives on the SQUARE, which has been prepared by the groundsman for a particular match. For some reason, 'cut' is only ever stuck in front of 'strip' when a bowler is having a SHOCKER, as in: 'Glenn McGrath was unable to locate even the cut strip.' It's a phrase England batsmen spent ten years dreaming of hearing.

See also METRONOME.

CUTLERY

The knife plays a surprisingly incisive role in the language of cricket, to say nothing of the spoon (a mis-hit stroke which often ends up in a fielder's lap) and the fork (the moment in a county cricketer's career when he must

Perhaps the reason we are always being told we don't see any late-cuts any more is that the batsmen are too busy swatting flies

decide whether to clog up the system for another year or retire gracefully and open a pub). But it is the knife which really cuts the metaphorical mustard. Knives can be out for a struggling captain, but can also be twisted moments after the selectors have offered a vote of confidence. The edge of the knife is where close matches are forever teetering, and if you need an implement with which to cut the tension, then look no further.

Knives exist beyond the realm of imagery too. In November 1998, the West Indies middle-order batsman Jimmy Adams flew home from South Africa almost as soon as he had arrived. According to team officials, Adams had cut his hand with a butter knife on the plane while trying to prise open a bread roll. Others reckoned he had been trying to prise apart bickering team-mates. He was probably grateful to miss the trip: West Indies lost all five Tests and six of the seven one-day internationals.

The South Africa wicketkeeper, Mark Boucher, was forced to sit out a game against Australia in August 2000 after slicing his fingers while hacking away at a particularly stubborn piece of biltong. And Alamgir Sheriyar pulled out of Kent's championship match against Surrey in 2003 after allegedly slicing a hand doing the washing-up, a story that raised eyebrows mainly at the thought of a county cricketer making himself useful in the kitchen.

Roy Gilchrist, the BEAMER-happy West Indian fast bowler, had no such excuses when he was sent home from the tour of India in 1958–59 for an unspecified knife incident. But perhaps the most surprisingly gratuitous piece of cutlery abuse came at LORD'S in 2004 when one member of the MCC threatened another with a knife for supposedly using a mobile phone in the members' area during the first Test between England and West Indies. Police were called, but the aggressor fled from the scene before presumably melting inconspicuously into the outside world with his straw boater and club tie.

DAVIS, GEORGE (1941–)

On 19 August 1975 George Davis became the first mini-cab driver from Ilford in Essex to help Australia win the ASHES. Just as uniquely, he was serving a seventeen-year sentence for armed robbery at the time. The scene had been set for an enthralling final day in the third Test at Headingley, where Australia, who needed a draw to retain the urn, were about to resume on 220 for 3 in pursuit of 445. But when the groundsman pulled back the covers, he discovered that the pitch had been gouged and oil poured on a good length. Graffiti on a wall proclaiming 'George Davis is innocent' explained all.

Four men were put on trial, and their leader, Peter Chappell, was jailed for eighteen months. But did they have a point? The following May, the home secretary, Roy Jenkins, overturned Davis's conviction after doubts arose about the evidence. It can only be assumed that England's captain, Tony Greig, failed to send Davis a bunch of flowers: after his Australian counterpart Ian Chappell (no relation) refused to play the last day of the Headingley Test on another strip, the game was abandoned as a draw and the Ashes remained in Aussie hands. Rain would probably have restricted England's chances of pushing for victory, but, hey, it's the principle that counts.

Even more frustratingly for England, Davis was then jailed two years after his release for involvement in another bank heist. In 1978, the Surrey punk band Sham 69 released a song called 'George Davis is Innocent', while Duran Duran's 1981 number 'Friends of Mine' included the line 'George Davis is coming out'. They were half right. Davis emerged from prison in 1984, only to return in 1987 for another misdemeanour.

DEATH

To bowl at the death means to bowl at the end of a one-day innings, when YORKERS and SLOWER BALLS are all the rage. It would be all too neat to report that death-bowling is a dying art. In fact, it is alive and kicking, and might alone explain why Darren Gough's international career was prolonged for as long as it was.

DECLARATIONS

The former Australia captain Mark Taylor called his auto-biography *Time to Declare*, but not all declaration decisions come with enough time to sit down and write a book (or at least sit down and talk to a journalist who writes it instead). Most Test captains who declare their team's innings closed do so from a position of strength bordering on the conservative. Occasionally, though – and to shivers of thinly disguised *Schadenfreude* from every-one else – the declaration goes spectacularly wrong.

To lose a Test after declaring once could be considered a cheap travesty of an over-used Oscar Wildism. To lose a Test after declaring twice is to invite despair that not even Wilde could have conjured a laugh out of. South Africa's Graeme Smith became the second captain to suffer this fate when, with his side needing to win the third and final Test at Sydney to square the series in

January 2006, he was forced by the weather to set Australia an overly friendly target.

But Smith's *faux pas* was a barely audible burp next to the ear-splitting belch emitted by Garry Sobers at Port-of-Spain in March 1968. After quite reasonably declaring West Indies' first innings on an apparently impregnable 526 for 7, he then closed the second on 92 for 2, which set England a target of 215 in 2¾ hours. They got there with three minutes to spare, and went on to win the series. Sobers was called all kinds of names by the locals – very few of them 'Garry' – but argued that England had shown no sign of scoring so quickly in the first three Tests, which were all drawn. He later branded the team-mates who had originally backed his decision, only to distance themselves from it later, as 'strangers to the truth'.

Poor old Sobers did not even get a shiny new leather jacket for his troubles. That was the gift given to Hansie Cronje by a bookmaker after he agreed to make a game of the fifth and final Test between South Africa and England at Centurion in January 2000. A slightly bemused Nasser Hussain was persuaded by Cronje to declare England's first innings at 0 for 0, before South Africa forfeited their second – something which often happened in county cricket but never before in a Test – to leave a target of 249 in 76 overs. England won by two wickets, but revelations five months later that Cronje had been motivated not so much by the good of the game as 53,000 rand and an addition to the family wardrobe shocked the world.

Other declarations have merely been misjudged. Graeme Hick barely spoke to Mike Atherton for the rest of England's tour of Australia in 1994–95 after Atherton declared England's second innings at Sydney with Hick on 98. He never did score an ASHES hundred. And when

Somerset's Brian Rose declared at 1 for 0 after one over of their Benson & Hedges Cup match against Worcestershire in 1979, he did not simply ignore the spirit of the game – he led it by the scruff of the neck to a motorway bridge and hurled it under the wheels of a passing lorry. Rose's plan – to deny Worcestershire the chance to improve their run-rate sufficiently to qualify for the quarter-finals ahead of Somerset – was legal. It just wasn't very ethical. Declarations had been allowed at any stage of any game since 1957, but Rose's sleight of mathematics led them to be banned in one-day cricket.

See also MATCH-FIXING.

DIBBLY-DOBBLY

An adjective which, when applied to a bowler of medium pace, can be both endearing and damning. At international level, dibbly-dobblers sacrifice speed for guile, are often prematurely balding and usually from New Zealand (at the 1992 World Cup, the Kiwi trio of Gavin Larsen, Chris Harris and Rod Latham were christened Dibbly, Dobbly and Wobbly). At club level, dibbly-dobblers are former fast bowlers who have decided to prolong their careers by settling for accuracy ahead of aggression. Amateur batsmen hate them. Fifteen-year-olds who are kept out of the team by them and forced to carry the drinks instead soon drift off into a life of DRUGS, crime and FOOTBALL. Forget absent fathers and happy-slappers: the dibbly-dobblers have got a lot to answer for.

See also BITS AND PIECES; METRONOME; MILITARY MEDIUM.

DISMISSALS

Bowlers always complain that cricket is a batsman's game, a whinge that fails to take into account that a batsman's innings is only ever one ball away from its potential conclusion. Even worse, a batsman can be dismissed in ten different ways, or eleven if you include 'retired out', which is entirely self-inflicted and occurs only in matches against the likes of Oxford University or the PCB Patron's XI. The ten modes of dismissal, in approximate descending order of regularity, are: caught, bowled, lbw (LEG BEFORE WICKET), run out, stumped, hit wicket, handled the ball, hit the ball twice, obstructing the field, and timed out.

The first five of these occur frequently, the sixth (hit wicket) rarely, and the last four hardly ever. In fact, by the end of 2005 the number of players who had been given out handled the ball in Test cricket had reached a mere seven, mainly because it usually requires a certain amount of stupidity on the part of the batsman. Andrew Hilditch, however, is exempt from blame. Standing innocently at the non-striker's end during the second Test between Australia and Pakistan at Perth in March 1979, Hilditch handed the ball back to the bowler Sarfraz Nawaz following a defensive shot from his opening partner Rick Darling. Scandalously, Sarfraz appealed and a flabbergasted Hilditch was given out, the victim of a revenge attack after Pakistan's No. 11 Sikander Bakht, had been vindictively run out earlier in the day for backing up too far.

The only Test batsman to be given out obstructing the field is Len Hutton, who in 1951 at The Oval tried to SWEEP a delivery from South Africa's Athol Rowan, an off-spinner whose run-up had been reduced to a couple of shuffles by a war-time bomb in the Western Desert.

The ball popped up off the bat handle and was about to be caught by the wicketkeeper Russell Endean when Hutton instinctively knocked it away. Having been denied a simple catch, Endean later became the first batsman in Test history to be given out handled the ball when he brushed aside a delivery that might have been heading for his stumps after he had thrust a pad at England's Jim Laker at Cape Town in January 1957.

At least Hutton and Endean made it on to the pitch. There have been three instances in FIRST-CLASS cricket of batsmen timed out under Law 31, which allows three minutes from the fall of a wicket for the new batsman 'to be in position to take guard or for his partner to be ready to receive the next ball'. The most recent example occurred at Trent Bridge in 2003 during the game between Nottinghamshire and Durham University Cricketing Centre of Excellence. The Notts No. 11, Andrew Harris, had not been expecting to bat because of a groin strain, but by the time he realized he was required in the middle, the Durham fielders were heading towards the pavilion.

Harris's plight pales into insignificance besides the fate of Thomas Sidwell, the Leicestershire wicketkeeper who in 1921 was given out 'absent, lost on Tube' after failing to resume his overnight innings of 1 not out against Surrey at The Oval. It was a single which Hanif Mohammad could have done with when he was run out for 499 in the last over of the day while playing for Karachi against Bahawalpur in 1958–59. Many years later, Hanif told the Pakistani journalist Qamar Ahmed that, with two balls of the day to go, the scoreboard had him on 496. His plan was to take a pair of twos to reach 500 by stumps, but he was run out off the penultimate ball of the session trying to sneak a second. Only when he was back in the pavilion did he realize that the board was wrong: he had been on 498. 'Those damn fool scorers got it wrong,' he is supposed to have remarked when Brian Lara broke his record with an unbeaten 501 for Warwickshire against Durham at Edgbaston in June 1994.

An even nastier twist lay in store for the man batting with Hanif at the time. In Karachi's next game their eighteen-year-old wicketkeeper, Abdul Aziz, was hit above the heart by an OFF-BREAK and retired hurt. Tragically, he never made it to hospital and his second-innings effort is recorded as 'did not bat, dead'. That this did not count against his AVERAGE will have been of little consolation.

Still, if bowlers really reckon it's a batsman's game, they should have been around in the seventeenth century, when batsmen were entitled to hit the ball as many times as they liked to avoid losing their wicket. This meant that close fielders often feared for their lives. Some were luckier than others. In 1624 Jasper Vinall died after being hit on the head by the bat of Edward Tye, who was damned if he was going to let Vinall catch him. The coroner, obviously deciding that the laws of cricket were above the laws of the land, returned a verdict of misadventure.

Then there was the strange case of the badly manufactured bail. When Pat Symcox was beaten by a Mushtaq Ahmed GOOGLY during the third Test at Faisalabad between Pakistan and South Africa in October 1997, he waited for the death rattle. And waited. And waited. Incredibly, the ball had passed between off stump and middle. 'Umpire Dunne gave his spectacles a disbelieving wipe, but the bail was found to be badly cut,' explained WISDEN with typical understatement.

See also MANKAD; MASTER THE; REARGUARD.

Tossed high into the air, the ideal donkey drop – a thing of unashamed pragmatism rather than beauty – will land directly on top of the stumps and leave the batsman first in two minds, then with a red face. But because donkey drops gratuitously remove the pitch from the equation, they are rightly spurned by any self-respecting bowler. In fact, their most famous purveyor did not even exist.

Tom Spedegue, the hero of a short story by Sir Arthur Conan Doyle, is an asthmatic teacher who practises his invention by lobbing a ball over a rope tied between two tall trees in the New Forest. Word of his deeds transcends the woodlands, and Spedegue ends up winning the ASHES for England, mainly because the Australians are unable to adapt their orthodox batting to the challenge. 'Every rule learned, every experience endured, had in a moment become useless,' wrote Conan Doyle. 'How could you play with a straight bat at a ball that fell from the clouds?' In the finest traditions of English medical care, Spedegue is immediately advised to retire by his doctor.

The Story of Spedegue's Dropper, published in 1929, was probably inspired by Conan Doyle's own experience of being duped by a donkey drop delivered by Alfred 'Bunny' Lucas, who won five Test caps for England between 1879 and 1884. Conan Doyle was so surprised by the delivery that, in trying to deal with it, he demolished two stumps with his bat before watching the ball land on the third.

Conan Doyle was no novice either. He played ten FIRST-CLASS matches for the MCC in the first decade of the twentieth century and was so thrilled to have dismissed W. G. GRACE – his only first-class wicket – that he remembered his fifteen minutes of fame by writing a seventy-stanza, mock-heroic poem. A convincing argument has it that the forename of his most famous creation, Sherlock Holmes, was an amalgam of the Nottinghamshire cricketers Frank Shacklock and Mordecai Sherwin, the latter a 17-stone wicketkeeper who also played in goal for Notts County. Sherlock's brother Mycroft is thought to have been inspired by the little-known Derbyshire siblings of the same name.

Real-life donkey droppers have disappeared from top-level cricket altogether now that the county championship has ditched three-day matches, which often required part-time bowlers to feed farcical runs to the batsmen in order to set up a DECLARATION on the last afternoon. The donkey drop – or a less vertiginous version – was one of the easiest ways of donating runs, and WISDEN relegates to a footnote centuries scored 'when FULL-TOSSES, LONG-HOPS etc were bowled deliberately to expedite a declaration'. For the withering 'etc' read 'donkey drops', the untouchables of cricket's caste system.

But it had once been considered a genuine wicket-taking delivery. The Leicestershire opener Maurice Hallam told Stephen Chalke how his team-mate Charles Palmer bamboozled batsmen in the 1940s and '50s with his own version of the ball: 'They went miles up in the air, into orbit. We're talking probably 20 feet. But his STRIKE-RATE was unbelievable. He hit the top of the stumps, people trod on their wicket or knocked the stumps down.'

Around the same time, the Somerset captain Jack Meyer toyed with donkey drops in county cricket after practising them while headmaster at Millfield School. But when Godfrey Evans, the Kent and England wicketkeeper, destroyed one of Meyer's overs by using a one-handed, tennis-racket grip, he quietly shelved the idea.

Since then, very few bowlers have had the nerve, or even the cheek, to dust it off, although there must be some doubt whether the donkey drops purveyed by Spedegue ('He was as accurate as a human howitzer pitching shells') would now be considered legal. Law 42.6 (b)(ii), which governs the 'Bowling of high full-pitched balls', states that 'A slow delivery which passes or would have passed on the full above shoulder height of the striker standing upright at the CREASE is to be deemed dangerous and unfair, whether or not it is likely to inflict physical injury on the striker.' As we speak, the Australians are probably calling for Spedegue's Test career to be declared null and void.

See also BEAMER.

DOOSRA

Hindi and Urdu for 'second' or 'other', the doosra is the off-spinner's retort to the leg-spinner's GOOGLY. The conventional OFF-BREAK turns in to the right-handed batsman, but the doosra goes the other way. If undetected it can wreak havoc, as England discovered against Muttiah Muralitharan on their tour of Sri Lanka in December 2003, although the legality of that particular delivery was questioned soon after. The doosra is supposed to have been introduced into cricket's vocabulary by the former Pakistan wicketkeeper Moin Khan. In games against non-Urdu-speaking teams, he would urge his team-mate Saqlain Mushtaq to bowl the doosra, and then watch with glee as a New Zealander or Englishman was caught behind playing down the wrong line. These days, everyone knows the meaning of the word, so Saqlain tried to throw the cat back among the pigeons by claiming he had invented a 'teesra', or 'third one'. Like Shane Warne's much-trumpeted variations on the straight one, the teesra was more probably kidology than anything else. But the doosra goes from strength to strength and was recently admitted into the *Oxford English Dictionary*

See also CHUCKING; ZOOTER.

DOT BALLS

A ball off which no run is scored, indicated by a dot in the scorebook. Captains unafraid of sounding nerdy will exhort their bowlers to 'join the dots' – a reference to the fact that a MAIDEN over (one containing six dot balls) is conveyed in the scorebook by an uppercase 'M', with both vertical strokes of the letter joining up three dots.

Dot balls sound boring – and should not be mentioned at all on a first date – but bowlers love them because they build up PRESSURE. The record for consecutive dot balls in a FIRST-CLASS match is held by the South Africa off-spinner Hugh Tayfield, who in January 1957 at Durban bowled 137 in succession against England: 119 in the first innings (when he took 1 for 21 in 24 eight-ball overs) and 18 more in the second (when he took 8 for 69).

Alan Ross captured the scene with typical elegance in *Cape Summer*: 'Tayfield was encouraged, rather than allowed, to bowl 14 maidens in a row, 9 of them to [Trevor] Bailey who pushed forward regardless of the length of the ball. For a whole hour Bailey neither envisaged nor made a scoring stroke . . . The sharp single had been discarded as a youthful frolic: the hypnotic maidens of Tayfield had become as soothing and necessary to Bailey as opium to a mandarin. It clouded over now, and Bailey appealed unsuccessfully against the light. It was like a bridge player with five quick tricks in his hand stubbornly calling "No Bid".'

Tayfield was almost beaten forty-two years later by Manish Majithia, who – according to Bill Frindall – did not concede a run for 136 balls while bowling for Madhya Pradesh against Railways at Indore in India's domestic competition, the Ranji Trophy. His second-innings figures were a remarkable 20-20-0-1.

See also DRUGS; JOURNALISM; REARGUARD; STREAKER; *TEST MATCH SPECIAL*.

DRIFT

Drift, like cops, can be good and bad. Good drift occurs when spinners get the ball to deviate in the air because of the revolutions they place on it with either their fingers or WRIST. Shane Warne's WONDERBALL to Mike Gatting remains the Platonic ideal. Gatting was lulled into thinking he was safe because the ball drifted further and further outside leg-stump before spitting back across him like a disgusted Millwall fan. Bad drift has nothing to do with spin bowling and everything to do with passive leadership. If a captain allows a game to drift, it means he is not being proactive enough/thinking on his feet/taking the bull by the horns. In fact, he is probably thinking in clichés.

DRUGS

For Shane Warne, it was a bitter pill to swallow. On the morning of Australia's opening game in the 2003 World Cup, Warne revealed he had tested positive for two banned diuretics, hydrochlorothiazide and amiloride, and would have plenty of time to practise their pronunciation on the flight home. He had been given the drugs, he said, by his mum Brigitte while trying to lose weight after making a swift return from a shoulder injury, although sceptics noted that diuretics could also be used to mask steroids. Most critics were happy to put Warne's behaviour down to vanity, but the authorities took a dimmer view and, when the second test confirmed the result of the first, banned him from all cricket for a year. Warne had to take the decision on the double-chin. But in a sport where performance-enhancing drug abuse is virtually unheard of, this was sensational news.

Yet it was not unprecedented. The New South Wales batsman Graeme Rummans was banned for a month in 2002 for taking the antibiotic probenecid, while a year earlier Duncan Spencer, the former Western Australia fast bowler once named by Viv Richards as one of the quickest he had ever faced, received an eighteen-month ban for taking nandrolone in an attempt to ease a long-standing back problem.

Further down the illegal-substance pecking-order, Ian Botham was banned for a year for the grave crime of smoking cannabis. On his return to the England side in August 1986, he had the New Zealand opener Bruce Edgar caught at slip with his very first ball, thus equalling Dennis Lillee's then world record of 355 Test wickets.

Touring teams are more likely to get into trouble than most, simply because they have so much time on their hands. Before he was captain of New Zealand, Stephen Fleming was banned for three matches, along with Dion Nash and Matthew Hart, after smoking marijuana on the tour of South Africa in 1994–95, while five members of the South African team – plus their physio – also made a hash of things after winning a Test match in Antigua in May 2001. All six were fined 10,000 rand. Phil Tufnell was more fortunate after staff at Bardelli's bar in Christchurch chucked him out for allegedly puffing away in the disabled toilets during England's tour of New Zealand in 1996–97. Tufnell was later found not guilty by the England management.

In fact, a more genuine den of drug-taking iniquity had always been closer to home. When the Warwickshire ALL-ROUNDER Paul Smith admitted in a newspaper article in 1996 that had he had taken ecstasy and cocaine during his career he was banned for twenty-two months – despite having already retired. The club responded by testing all their players, and promptly found traces of cannabis in the sample from the wicketkeeper, Keith Piper, who was suspended for one match. So what did Warwickshire do next? That's right, they signed Ed Giddins, the former Sussex SWING bowler who had just served a twenty-month ban of his own – for taking cocaine.

Years later, Warwickshire's drug culture hit the head-lines once more. Their former captain Dermot Reeve admitted he had been fighting a cocaine addiction, while their England A all-rounder, the 21-year-old Graham Wagg, was sacked for dabbling in the same drug. And if that wasn't enough, Piper was then banned again for more cannabis use. Some were outraged; others pointed out less high-handedly that such substances could hardly improve your straight-drives, SLOWER BALLS or slip catches. But the message was clear. Forget trips to the moon: for an experience that was almost literally out of this world, the place to be was Edgbaston.

Alas, this revelation came too late to save the Melbourne-based fan who was arrested in 1999 for selling drugs to feed his dangerous cricket-memorabilia habit. Police who raided the home of Paul Sullivan found not only a stash of cannabis, but bats reportedly signed by Don BRADMAN and Brian Lara. The judge ordered him to hand over his ill-gotten cricketana – a lesson for us all.

DUCK

Just as tennis has its own special name for zero (which is shaped like an egg: love comes from *l'oeuf*), so cricket seeks to ease the pain of a batsman's failure to score even a single run by calling it something else altogether. Duck is actually a shortened form of duck's egg, and coincidentally rhymes with a word which batsmen might mutter if they score one. In Australia, the humiliation is heightened by the presence of Channel 9's Daddles the Duck, who waddles – with a quack that says 'kill me' – across the screen while the batsman trudges back to the pavilion.

Cricket being cricket, it has not been content simply to call a duck a duck. The *Guardian* journalist Frank Keating began an article about ducks for *Wisden Cricket Monthly* like this: 'Duck, blob, blonger, globe, glozzer, quacker, zoink, zebedee, the "tin-o" . . . zero, nought . . . there are still a lot about, "untroubling" the scorers.'

Just as typically, ducks come in all shapes and sizes. To register a golden duck means you have been dismissed by the first ball you have faced. A pair (of spectacles) means you have scored two ducks in the same game. A king pair means both ducks were golden. There is some dispute over the meaning of a diamond duck, which occurs either when a batsman is out to the first ball of a team's innings, or when he is run out without facing. And we will spare ourselves a great deal of effort if we don't even begin to speculate on the exact nature of a platinum duck, let alone whether it actually exists.

What we can say for sure is that the better the player, the louder the quack. Graham Gooch began his Test career in 1975 with a pair against Australia at Edgbaston, while the prolific Jimmy Cook fell to the first ball of South Africa's first home Test in 1992 after twenty-two years of apartheid-induced isolation. Don BRADMAN's second-ball duck in his final innings in 1948 rates as one of the most dramatic moments in any sport, along with the first ball he faced during the 1932–33 BODYLINE series. Trying to PULL a Bill Bowes LONG-HOP, Bradman bottom-edged the ball on to his stumps, prompting what his batting partner Jack Fingleton later described as 'an unbelievable hush of calamity, for men refused to believe what their eyes had seen'. India's Ajit Agarkar earned the nickname Bombay Duck after recording five blobs/glozzers/zoinks in a row on a tour of Australia to equal the Aussie leg-spinner Bob Holland's Test record. When Kim Hughes captained the rebel Australians to South Africa in 1985–86 he made a king pair in the third unofficial Test at Johannesburg, but got a third chance when he emerged as a runner for Rodney Hogg. He was run out first ball. Almost as gallingly, Russel Arnold registered two ducks in the space of seventy-five minutes during Sri Lanka's tour game against Hampshire in August 1998.

But that was an age compared to Peter Judge's efforts for Glamorgan against the touring Indians in June 1946. When Judge was last man out in Glamorgan's first innings, bowled first ball by the leg-spinner Chandra Sarwate, India enforced the FOLLOW-ON. With time running out, Judge hung around to open Glamorgan's second innings, whereupon Sarwate bowled him first ball again. It is technically impossible to achieve a faster pair than that.

Anyone who scores a duck in any form of the game is eligible to join the Primary Club, a cricketing charity that raises money for the visually impaired and currently boasts over 12,500 members. Its patron is the former England left-arm spinner Derek Underwood, who once scored two ducks in a day for Kent against South Africa so is ideally placed to lead from the front. For more information write to: The Primary Club, PO Box 12121, Saffron Walden, Essex CB10 2ZF, or phone +44 (0)1799 586507.

See also INVINCIBLES; PACKER, KERRY.

DUCKWORTH/LEWIS METHOD, THE

Rarely have two mild-mannered, middle-aged statisticians been so reviled as Frank Duckworth and Tony Lewis. Their crime? To produce an extremely fair system of recalculating targets in RAIN-affected one-day matches. Unfortunately, the system requires a calculator and possibly a pen, which has upset those accustomed to using an abacus, a chisel and a slab of stone. Some of these dinosaurs have even muttered darkly about walking through the streets of Leicester and Northampton brandishing effigies of the editor of the Royal Statistical Society's monthly news magazine and the lecturer in mathematical subjects at the University of the West of England. But they have been too busy grappling with, well, Duckworth/Lewis.

The usual gripe about the D/L method is that you need a degree in maths to work it out. Since this tends to come from journalists who have a full print-out of D/L calculations in front of them, it can usually be put down to the foul mood caused by the following sequence of events: it is 10pm, the one-day game they are covering between the Scottish Saltires and the Derbyshire Phantoms has just been affected by the weather for third time, and their editors are screaming down the phone for their report.

The truth is that D/L is by far the fairest system yet devised, even if it goes beyond the realms of mental arithmetic. While previous systems loaded the dice too heavily in favour of one side or the other, D/L bases its calculations on the idea that each side, at any given point in its one-day innings, has two sets of resources available: wickets and overs. From there stems an infinite number of possible combinations, each of them checkable on a handy chart. Examples can be provided on a stamped addressed envelope containing a large blank cheque. Suffice to say, the system works.

Which is not the same thing as saying that it never leads to disaster. South Africa were knocked out of their own World Cup in 2003 after their rain-affected match with Sri Lanka at Durban finished in a TIE. Had the D/L requirements been posted for all to see on the Kingsmead scoreboard, the South African batsmen Mark Boucher and Lance Klusener would have realized they needed to take a single off the last ball they faced before rain caused the game to be cancelled. But a message from the dressing-room was not conveyed properly to the middle, and Boucher defended the crucial delivery to midwicket. When the error was realized, a nation slapped its forehead. And, somewhere in England, two well-meaning statisticians might have gulped hard.

See also FIELDING POSITIONS; SHOCKER.

ECONOMY

In cricket, cheapness is a virtue. Bowlers with good economy rates are adept not so much at fiddling their match expenses as keeping the runs down, and can win one-day games with their meanness alone. The meanest of them all was Joel Garner, the 6ft 8in West Indian known as Big Bird who conceded a barely believable 3.09 runs per over in ninety-eight one-day internationals. The fact that the next-best economy rate is 3.28 – by England's Bob Willis – highlights Garner's genius, which was based on disconcerting bounce and a deadly YORKER. In all, only thirty men with fifty or more one-day international wickets had gone for under four runs an over by the start of 2006, and most of them played in the days before PINCH-HITTING became an integral part of the game. In an era when many players are prepared to cheat to gain an advantage, being economical with the ball is a skill second only to being economical with the truth.

See also METRONOME.

EXTRAS

If the batsmen's individual scores tell you something about how well the bowlers have performed, then the extras at the bottom of the scorecard reflect the bowlers' – and to a lesser extent, the wicketkeeper's – discipline or lack of it. Byes (runs scored after the ball has failed to touch anything), leg-byes (runs scored when the ball has come off a part of the batsman's body other than his gloves), wides (when the batsman can't reach the ball), and no-balls (when no part of the bowler's foot is behind the popping CREASE) make up the traditional quartet of what the Australians call 'sundries'. Penalty runs (five added in one go for various offences) were introduced much later and are still rare.

In a transparent attempt to make extras interesting, stat-isticians compile lists of highest-this and most-that (some of them even give extras an upper-case 'E'). Did you know the most extras in a single Test innings was the 71 (b21, lb8, w4, nb38) conceded by West Indies against Pakistan at Georgetown in April 1988? Or that the highest Test total without a bye was Sri Lanka's 713 for 3 against Zimbabwe at Bulawayo in May 2004, when the wicketkeeper was the 21-year-old Tatenda Taibu. It would be nice to think that Taibu's agility behind the stumps was the main reason for the record, but the awful truth is that a weakened Zimbabwe attack never passed the bat often enough to make him earn his keep. In fact, the bowling was so bad that six Zimbabweans conceded over 100 runs each – the first time this had happened in the history of Test cricket.

When very little else is happening in the world of cricket, someone somewhere calls for the abolition of the leg-bye, and does so in such ringing tones that you might think he was demanding an end to Third World sweat-shops. The argument, a perfectly sound one, is put forward that the batting side should not be rewarded when the batsman has failed to hit the ball. Everyone agrees that this is an absurd state of affairs, and then does nothing about it. Pity Martyn Moxon. Playing for England against

New Zealand at Auckland in February 1988, he was denied three runs by the umpire when a SWEEP shot was wrongly signalled as leg-byes. Moxon later fell for 99. It remained his highest Test score.

See also NERVOUS NINETIES; SHOCKER.

FANCY-DRESS

Post-modern irony has rarely found much expression in cricket, but the relatively recent phenomenon of fancy-dress suggests all is not lost. At every English Test venue other than LORD's – where the sartorial crimes are committed by members of the MCC – the seats are filled by nuns, Vikings, Richie BENAUDS, and Sylvester the Cats. The relationship between these japesters – who range from stag-do revellers to City boys on the lash – and the ground authorities has at times been strained. During the 1997 ASHES Test at Headingley, a university lecturer dressed as a carrot was frogmarched out of the ground for what the authorities called 'drunken and abusive behaviour'. Mr Brian Cheesman, who had been dressing up for the Leeds Test since 1982, denied the charge. In the same game, a stray pantomime cow was RUGBY-tackled so ferociously by stewards that the man making up the rear end had to be taken to hospital. Fountain-like supplies of alcohol can usually be relied upon to dull the pain, but these days pitch invasions by giant vegetables and bovines with theatrical pretensions are frowned upon.

See also AGRICULTURE; STREAKERS.

*Lord Harris hilariously dressed as a member of
cricket's aristocracy*

FEATHERBED

A batsman's paradise and a bowler's living hell, the feather-bed is a pitch which is so flat you could easily doze off on it. Such luxuries are rarely found in England, where sleeping on the job is limited to the House of Lords, and where pitches which are helpful to the seamers provide handy excuses for the batsmen. No, for the sort of feather-bed which would encourage you to plump up your pillow and order the morning papers, try the Recreation Ground in the Antiguan capital of St John's. It was the scene of Brian Lara's two world-record innings against England (375 in 1993–94 and 400 not out a decade later), and in recent years has provided the run-starved West Indians with some AVERAGE-fattening succour. In May 2002 they racked up 629 for 9 against India, and followed that in May 2003 by successfully chasing a target of 418 to beat Australia. No side had ever scored more runs in the fourth innings to win a Test. In April 2004 came Lara's unbeaten quadruple-century out of a total of 751 for 5, the highest ever conceded by England. And a year later the opener Chris Gayle helped himself to 317 against South Africa as West Indies amassed 747. Bowlers picked for Tests in Antigua might prefer to pull a muscle in the shower before the game.

See also SHIRTFRONT.

FERRET

A batsman so bad that he is said to 'go in after the RABBITS'. Also very fond of DUCKS.

FIELDING POSITIONS

It will gall those who regard the language of cricket as only slightly less intelligible than Swahili to learn that most of the terms used to describe fielding positions are rooted in logic. Mid-off, for example, is midway to the BOUNDARY on the off-side, and is in chatting distance of mid-on, his mirror image on the on- or leg-side. Five minutes at a game will be enough to learn that mid-off and mid-on, often the weakest fielders in the side, stand trembling at the outer limits of the area known as THE V. Midwicket loiters on the leg-side on an imaginary line drawn from the middle of the wicket, while square-leg is the man standing square of the wicket on the leg-side, rather than the one with the clubfoot. The sweeper sweeps up anything that beats the infield on the off-side boundary. Adjectives denote distance from the bat: deep and long are far away, silly and short are close in, and fine is, well, fine. There are, though, exceptions to the logic rule of thumb:

- Slips: the first over of a Test match will usually see three of them standing next to the wicketkeeper, waiting for a slip by the batsman. It is one of the hardest jobs in cricket: unlike the keeper, the slips go gloveless; and unlike the keeper, who often gets to catch edges that barely deviate off the straight, the slips need to have more than a passing acquaintance with cricket's angles. The rarely seen fly-slip waits between the slips and the boundary and was a genuine catching position when Alan Knott was batting.
- Point: the fielder who stands square on the off-side on an imaginary line drawn from the popping-

CREASE. Point used to field right under the point of the bat, but these days he has retreated to a safer distance, and left such foolhardiness to the man now known as silly point.

- Cover: the fielder who stands in front of square on the off-side, not far from point. The cover region is so called because it usually gets covered when the RAIN arrives. Extra cover lends a helping hand.
- Gully: the fielder who inhabits the gap, or gully, between the slips and point.
- Third man: the man who skulks on the fence behind the batsman on the off-side. He used to be called 'third man up', because he would help out slip and point, but now he barely exists at all, causing apoplexy among older observers who like to tot up the number of runs third man would have saved had he been in position.

See also AGRICULTURE; BOX; CORDON.

FIRST-CLASS

A compliment, yes, but part of cricket's love of classification too. No game can be deemed first-class unless it is scheduled to take place over at least three days on a proper turf pitch at a suitably high-standard venue, contains eleven players a side, and is sanctioned by the home board. This means that while a three-day extended NET session between Loughborough University and a second-string Somerset side counts as first-class, a one-day international between India and Pakistan does not. Statisticians are forever squabbling about the starting-point of first-class cricket, although 1801 seems to be the general favourite.

FISHING

Both cricket and fishing contain a certain amount of waiting around for the right moment to pounce, but cricket clearly fancies itself as the more patient pastime. Why else would batsmen intemperate enough to play away from their body and dangle their bat outside off-stump be said to be fishing, as if fishing were the height of recklessness?

FLANNELS

When Rudyard Kipling sneered in his 1902 poem 'The Islanders' at 'the flannelled fools at the wicket', he was harking back to the days when a cricketer's trousers were still made out of flannel, an era which can reduce Englishmen of a certain disposition to red-eyed wrecks. By the middle of the nineteenth century, flannel had given way to cotton, but, well, cricket trousers were known as flannels, and that was that. Today's synthetic efforts retain the name. No self-respecting socialite would be seen dead in a pair of flannels nowadays, unless he were hobnobbing at a cricketing fundraiser. But back in the 1930s, the British-born Hollywood actor Charles Aubrey Smith, who captained England to victory over South Africa at Port Elizabeth in his only Test in March 1889 and went on to form the Hollywood Cricket Club, would often attend the HCC dances in his pristine whites. Strange how the sport never really caught on in America.

See also COFFIN; USA.

Ostensibly playing an off-drive, Surrey and England's Frank Druce ends up demonstrating how to fish

FLASH

Flashing is not generally recommended, in either of the colloquial senses of the term. Its less obvious meaning is to chase a wide ball outside off-stump, but – as commentators never tire of telling us – if you're going to flash, then flash hard. The thinking behind this wearily doled-out piece of advice is that any edge will be more difficult to catch than if the batsman had flashed softly, which probably isn't possible anyway.

See also STREAKERS.

FLAT-TRACK BULLY

Just as it was hard to look at the former leader of the Conservatives Michael Howard in the same light after his colleague Ann Widdecombe said he had 'something of the night' about him, so Graeme Hick was indelibly scarred when John Bracewell called him a 'flat-track bully'. Bracewell was referring not only to the ten centuries Hick made while spending two winters at the end of the 1980s with Northern Districts in New Zealand – where the bowling was as friendly as the people – but to his tendency to fail in Test cricket when England needed him most. The term has since been used to describe any batsman who succeeds only when conditions are in his favour.

See also BOUNCER.

FLIPPER

One of the many weapons in the leg-spinner's armoury, and one of the hardest to get right. The flipper is squeezed out of the front of the hand from between the thumb and first two fingers, and skids on to the batsman more quickly than expected. Shane Warne bamboozled many an Englishman with his flipper during the 1990s, but the inventor of the delivery was the New Zealand-born Clarrie Grimmett, who moved to Australia in his early twenties and ended up taking 216 wickets in only thirty-seven Tests for his adopted country. Grimmett spent years perfecting the delivery, and when batsmen began to pick it by listening for the tell-tale snap of his spinning fingers, he began clicking the digits on his left hand just to confuse them.

See also WONDERBALL; ZOOTER.

FOLLOW-ON

Either a noun (with a hyphen), or a verb (without). To follow on is to have shown utter ineptitude with the bat, since it means you have failed to get within a certain amount of runs of the opposition's first-innings score (200 in a five-day Test match, 150 in three- or four-day domestic cricket). Assuming the captain of the fielding side so wishes, you then have to bat again immediately, with the possibility that you might lose by an innings. In other words, your team's two innings do not even add up to their team's one. Then again, if you can win a Test after following on, immortality is guaranteed. At the time of writing, this feat had been achieved only three times: all three against Australia, twice by England, and once in each of the nineteenth, twentieth and twenty-first centuries.

The first occasion took place at Sydney in 1894–95, when England were asked to bat again by Jack Blackham after scoring 325 in reply to Australia's 586. Second time round England managed 437, which left Australia needing 177 to win. England thought the game was lost, but their captain, Andrew Stoddart, who would take his own life twenty-one years later, ordered his slow left-armer Bobby Peel under a cold shower – the precursor, perhaps, to Sir Alex Ferguson's hairdryer treatment – and next morning watched him take six wickets on a pitch spiced up by heavy overnight RAIN. England won by ten runs.

In 1981, at Headingley, they did it again in a match whose fame is to cricket what the Rumble in the Jungle is to heavyweight boxing and Red Rum to the Grand National. England were 135 for 7 in their second innings and still needed another 92 merely to make Australia bat again. The team had checked out of its hotel, while two Australian players – Dennis Lillee and Rod Marsh – had sent their coach driver to place a bet on an England victory at odds of 500–1. It was then that Ian Botham, who had just lost his job as captain, decided to 'give it some humpty'. He added 117 with Graham Dilley, a further 67 with Chris Old, and finally 37 with Bob Willis. Set 130 for victory, Australia crumbled from 56 for 1 to 111 all out, with Willis taking 8 for 43 before sprinting off the field in a wild-eyed trance, a look which regular viewers of Sky's coverage believe he never quite managed to shake off.

The third miracle took place at Kolkata in March 2001, when Australia looked almost certain to extend their world-record winning sequence to seventeen Tests. Trailing by 274 on first innings, India were 232 for 4 in their second when Rahul Dravid walked out to join V. V. S. Laxman, who was on 95. The pair batted for more than a day to add an almighty 376, with Laxman eventually hitting 281 and Dravid 180. A shell-shocked Australia needed 384 but got nowhere near. Lightning had struck for the third time, and Australia understandably developed a complex about enforcing the follow-on.

Perhaps the most amazing win of them all took place in 1922, when Warwickshire played Hampshire at Edgbaston in a match which *WISDEN* described as 'surely without precedent in first-class cricket'. Batting first, Warwickshire made 223, before bundling Hampshire out for just 15, still their lowest-ever score. Hampshire, captained by Lionel Hallam (better known as the third Baron Tennyson and grandson of the Poet Laureate Alfred), then made 521 following on and proceeded to wrap up a 155-run victory by skittling Warwickshire for 158. According to the Hampshire No. 3, Harry Day, 'His Lordship led us to the train for Northampton. We all settled down until it was realised his ordered menu had not been heard of, so at a rush we ran for the Southampton train. Bottles popped and the carriage rocked all the way through southern England.'

See also ALL-ROUNDERS; MATCH-FIXING; QUEEN, THE; STICKY WICKET; WRISTS.

FOOTBALL

Strange sport where two teams can battle it out for ninety minutes (120, if you include extra-time) and the game can still end in a draw! Cricket lovers like to refer to it as 'soccer', just to wind soccer fans up. In fact, it properly belongs under 'S'.

See also RUGBY.

FRENCH CRICKET

Grossly simplified version of the real thing played mainly on the beach by sunburnt Brits. Bowlers try to hit the batsman's legs, but have to aim UNDERARM and deliver the sand-encrusted, sea-soaked ball from wherever it was last fielded. Batsmen are not allowed to move their feet, which, Australians might argue, would make Marcus Trescothick a natural.

Yet France's links with cricket actually deserve better than this Bank Holiday ritual. They are the reigning Olympic silver-medal holders, following the defeat of All Paris in the Vélodrome de Vincennes by the touring Devon & Somerset Wanderers (the wilfully misleading title given to a team made up of members of the Castle Cary Cricket Club in Somerset and former pupils of Blundell's School in Tiverton). OK, so the game took place in 1900. And the silver medal bit is dodgy too: Olympic medals did not exist until 1908, so they had to make do with tacky models of the Eiffel Tower instead. And they were made of bronze, not silver (the silver versions were awarded to the English). Oh, and most of the French team were English ex-pats. But you get the idea (the Olympic movement didn't, and cricket never appeared in the Games again).

There have even been heretical claims that France invented the game. In 2002, M. Didier Marchois, a former president of the French Cricket Federation and a member of the Chauny team, claimed that documents had been found which referred to matches played during the Hundred Years War near the battlefields of Crécy and Agincourt. 'They leave no room for doubt,' he argued unconvincingly. 'Cricket was born in the north of France and taken across the Channel by English soldiers who picked it up from us during truce periods.' A Yale professor was immediately wheeled out to prove that cricket had actually started in the south-east of England about 400 years ago – and a nation breathed a sigh of relief. Only when Captain Jean Arthur Albert BENAUD, Richie's great-great-something-or-other, arrived in Australia on the *Ville de Bordeaux* in 1840 could the French really claim to have connected with cricket. Today, Richie is the patron of France Cricket and even has a holiday home near Nice.

In 1997, the year he took up his post, France won the European Nations Cup, beating Germany in a nail-biting final by one run. The decisive single in the French innings turned out to be a leg-bye which ricocheted off the batsman's forehead and left him with a fractured skull. David Bordes spent two weeks in hospital.

Perhaps unnerved by French success, little Englanders prefer to dwell on the beautifully patronizing observation made by the historian G. M. Trevelyan about the French Revolution. 'If the French *noblesse* had been capable of playing cricket with their peasants,' he opined, 'their chateaux would never have been burnt.' But a journalist who covered the Devon & Somerset Wanderers' tour of France in 1900 – they played two other games on top of the Olympic showdown – felt the French were 'too excitable to enjoy the game'. He went on to claim that 'no Frenchman could be persuaded to play more than once. A cricketer in France is a stranger in a strange land looked upon with mingled awe and contempt by the average Frenchman.'

So there you have it: European history could have been radically altered if only our friends across *La Manche* had learned to appreciate the value of a good forward defensive.

See also EXTRAS; ORIGINS.

FULL-TOSS

There is not much to say about the full-toss – a ball which doesn't bounce before it reaches the batsman – except it's not a very good idea if you're a bowler.

See also BUFFET; HALF-VOLLEY; LONG-HOP.

GALLOWS

The type of humour that sustained a generation of England fans and allowed them to hurl witticisms at Australian fielders, despite the fact that another ASHES series had just been hopelessly surrendered. The gallows were also the setting for the only known execution of a Test cricketer. Leslie Hylton, a Jamaican who played six times for West Indies in the 1930s, was hanged in 1955 for the murder of his wife.

GARDENING

Often during his innings a batsman will walk down the pitch and prod it with his bat. He is gardening. He might do this for several reasons:

- To combat indentations caused by the ball on a damp pitch. If left to bake in the sun, the indentations can harden and create an uneven surface for the bowlers to exploit. Usually, the problems exist only in the batsman's mind, but occasionally they are very real. New Zealand beat England at Auckland in 2002 in precisely these circumstances (well, excuses are good for the soul).
- To regain his concentration after a loose shot. A short stroll down the pitch, head down so as not to get into a needless staring match with a fielder, followed

by a gentle pat of bat on turf – this ritual works wonders.

- To create an area of ROUGH on the pitch for the spin bowler in his own side to exploit later in the game. After pretending to even out some mystery bump with his bat, he turns vigorously on his heel, pirouetting his studs into the pitch and disturbing the surface. Technically, this is cheating, but it is very hard to police because a gentle amble down the pitch is not illegal. As a result, everyone does it.

- To make a sarcastic point about the bowler's tedious overuse of the short-pitched delivery. A method perfected by Ian Botham, this involves walking more than halfway down the 22-yard pitch and gardening ostentatiously in full view of the umpire. The point of this rather obvious joke is to remind everyone that the ball keeps pitching in the bowler's half. Still, it usually gets a chuckle from everyone except the bowler.

- To waste time, often to ensure that the fielding side are unable to squeeze in another over before LUNCH, TEA, or the close. There is, of course, absolutely nothing wrong with the pitch at all.

- To convince himself that the piece of wood he is holding actually serves a purpose. If he is failing to connect with the ball on a regular basis, gardening might be the only option.

- To do, well, a spot of gardening. He has noticed a rare but poisonous weed and wants to destroy it before the weed destroys everything else.

With a defensive technique like that, it's no wonder WG was always replacing the bails

GATE

The gap between bat and pad which drives coaches to distraction (and through which, on a bad day, coaches could be driven). To be gated is to be bowled through the gap, and thus to have your batting technique called into question. It is generally considered a bad career move, as is ramrodding the GRACE Gates at LORD'S.

See also WICKET.

GLANCE

If the martial art of aikido seeks to harness the strength of your opponent rather than to resist it, then the glance, or leg-glance, is cricket's riposte. Used to greatest effect against the quicker bowlers, it involves opening the face of the bat at the right moment so the pace of the ball sends it to the fine-leg fence. In this sense, it taps into the aikido principle of non-dissension: it is a piece of deflection rather than an act of aggression. Perhaps because of the heavier bats used today, as well as modern cricket's *lingua franca* of power and intimidation, the glance is not as popular as it was when Ranjitsinhji turned it into an art form at the start of the twentieth century.

'It is necessary to husband one's strength when one is engaged in continuous first-class cricket,' wrote Ranji in his famous *Jubilee Book of Cricket*, sounding not unlike Yoda. 'There is no doubt that when straight good-length balls are gently removed towards the leg-BOUNDARY by means of this stroke the bowler is liable to be much annoyed: he often loses his temper, then his head, and then his control over the ball.'

Ranji husbands his strengths

Ranji, an Indian nobleman known to his Cambridge colleagues as Smith, went on to win fifteen caps for England before getting his own back on his university mates by becoming Colonel His Highness Shri Sir Ranjitsinhji Vibhaji, Maharajah Jam Saheb of Nawanag, and working in the League of Nations. But it was his delicate turn of the WRISTS for which he is best remembered, a flexibility that would encourage writers to reach for the purple ink. Neville Cardus, the purplest of the lot, described him as 'the midsummer night's dream of cricket'.

See also ALBANIA; GOLDEN AGE; JOURNALISM; PURPLE PATCH.

GLOOM

'Bad light stopped play' is cricket's answer to *coitus interruptus*, and only marginally less frustrating. Generally, umpires lead the players off the field at the first sign of fading light, but there have been exceptions. England won a Test match in virtual darkness at Karachi in December 2000, then lost one at Auckland in April 2002 after the umpires agreed to use floodlights under the full moon. Naturally they felt justice had been done in the first case, and not in the second. But no word sums up cricket's melancholic relationship with the elements quite like gloom. And if you are very lucky, you will even see it prefaced with the adjective 'Stygian' (from the river Styx in the Greek underworld), a cliché which flatters writers into using it because of its classical heritage.

See also GARDENING; LIGHT METERS.

GOD

If God had been a cricketer (and there have been plenty of cricketers who have thought they were God), he would probably have batted at No. 4, bowled leg-spin, and fielded at backward point. He might even have kept wicket off his own bowling, upheld his own appeals, made the TEA and, after a few pints of nectar to celebrate England's twenty-seventh successive ASHES victory, moved in mysterious ways back to his hotel room.

Instead, God's influence on cricket has been second-hand (or first-hand, if you believe – as many do when it suits them – in a creator who intervenes in tight run-out decisions). Here, nation by nation, are some of the players who might have tried to seek divine inspiration:

- Australia: Few players use up so much energy in crossing themselves as Matthew Hayden, who has a bigger chest than most. But not everyone is enamoured with his very personal brand of muscular Christianity, which juxtaposes signs of the crucifix with pieces of advice to opposition batsmen that you won't find in the Bible. Brian Booth, who won 29 caps in the 1960s, later became one of the only players to be published on religion when he wrote *Cricket and Christianity*.

- England: David Sheppard captained his country in two of his twenty-two Tests, but became more famous as the Bishop of Liverpool, at the age of forty-six the youngest diocesan bishop ever appointed. After leaving the sport aged thirty-four to concentrate on religion he wrote that it was 'not so much a case of giving up cricket as of taking up something else which is infinitely worthwhile' – as if cricket somehow lagged in importance behind the afterlife. Since then, the England dressing-room has generally been a Godless place, although Graham Thorpe revealed in his autobiography, *Rising from the Ashes*, how he discovered faith following a traumatic split from his wife. 'Had you told me several years ago that Graham Thorpe might want to pray, I would have laughed at you,' he wrote, sounding worryingly like a deity himself. The closest most of his team-mates have come to a religious experience was when Buddhist monks tried to storm the Sinhalese Sports Club stadium in Colombo during the third Test against Sri Lanka in December 2003. The monks were angry that the match had not been stopped out of respect for the Venerable Gangodavila Soma Thera, who had died the previous week.

- India: Traditionally the most religiously diverse of all the Test nations. India's captains have included countless Hindus, as well as Christians (Vijay Hazare and Chandu Borde), Parsis (Polly Umrigar and Nari Contractor), Muslims (Ghulam Ahmed and Moham-mad Azharuddin) and a Sikh (Bishan Bedi). In his novel *The Moor's Last Sigh*, Salman Rushdie even makes use of an incident that occurred at Bombay in January 1960, when the Muslim batsman Abbas Ali Baig received a kiss from a sari-clad Hindu girl as he was walking off the field after scoring a half-century against Australia.

- New Zealand: The Kiwis think of their country as 'Godzone' (God's own), which is strange consider-ing their religious devotion to the cult of the All Blacks. Still, that hasn't stopped their zany official

Billy Bowden from describing God as his 'third umpire'.

- Pakistan: Ever since the death of the former opener Saeed Anwar's daughter in 2001, the Pakistanis have made Islam one of the defining aspects of their dressing-room. Beards appeared on the chins of Anwar, Inzamam-ul-Haq, Mushtaq Ahmed and Saqlain Mushtaq, while Yousuf Youhana forsook Christianity to become Mohammad Yousuf. At the height of the MATCH-FIXING crisis, when accusing fingers were being pointed almost at random, it became fashionable for Pakistani players to say they would swear their innocence on the Koran. Danish Kaneria, the sole Hindu in the side and only the second member of his religion to play for his country, claims not to feel left out.

- South Africa: Hansie Cronje's fall from grace was all the more poignant because of his involvement with the Dutch Reformed Church, a pillar of the South African Protestant community. Cronje rediscovered religion when a young girl was killed after running out in front of the car he was driving, and his inspirational captaincy of South Africa involved running Bible-discussion groups with several of his teammates. After Cronje's involvement with the bookies was finally exposed, he told the King Commission: 'In a moment of stupidity and weakness I allowed Satan and the world to dictate terms to me. The moment I took my eyes off Jesus my whole world turned dark.' He died in a plane crash in June 2002.

- Sri Lanka: Sanath Jayasuriya says Buddhist prayers twice a day to help him relax, while the fast bowler Chaminda Vaas does a mellifluous line in Catholic love songs. Both sets of beliefs are quietly forgotten when the two left-armers are appealing for lbw from over the wicket.

- West Indies: The gleaming crucifix of the former fast bowler Wes Hall used to mesmerize batsmen as he sprinted to the CREASE in the 1960s, but this was no bling. Hall later became an ordained minister, and might well have spent much of his time praying for the current West Indies side.

See also FIELDING POSITIONS; SLEDGING.

GOLDEN AGE

A halcyon period in cricketing history between 1890 and 1914 which evokes names such as W. G. GRACE, C. B. Fry, Ranji and Gilbert Jessop, and has been romanticized to death ever since. Not everyone agrees with the glowing epithet. Fred Trueman would probably argue that cricket's true Golden Age took place between 1952 and 1965, which happens to coincide with his England career. Others believe that WG would not have lasted five seconds in the modern era, when super slo-mos would surely have caught him replacing the bails behind the umpire's back. But the pre-First World War Golden Age satisfies the sport's almost innate desire to believe in a time when the phrase 'It's not cricket' indicated that the person saying it was a man of moral probity rather than a self-important halfwit. As such, it plays a crucial part in the game's mythology.

See also ALBANIA; ALL-ROUNDERS; GLANCE.

'Poor old googly!' swooned Bernard Bosanquet in *The Morning Post* in 1924. 'It has been subjected to ridicule, abuse, contempt, incredulity, and survived them all.' These days the googly – an OFF-BREAK disguised as a LEG-BREAK – is guaranteed to raise a chuckle simply because it sounds faintly rude. But at the turn of the twentieth century, it was as serious as the Schleswig-Holstein Question and, as far as batsmen were concerned, just as impenetrable.

Bosanquet invented the delivery during a game of Twisti-Twosti, the aim of which was to bounce a tennis ball across a table in such a way that your opponent, sitting at the other end, could not catch it. Since Bosanquet studied at Eton and Oxford, he had plenty of time to perfect the art of sending the ball first one way, then the other, but with no discernible change of action. The result became known as the googly (or Bosie, or wrong 'un), and played a major role in England's ASHES victory of 1903–04, when Bosanquet took 6 for 51 during the decisive fourth Test at Sydney. In 1905 he returned figures of 8 for 107 in the defeat of Australia at Trent Bridge, but he quit soon after with only seven caps to his name.

Batsmen everywhere breathed a sigh of relief, even if England got a nasty taste of their own medicine in South Africa, where a trio of googly bowlers – Bert Vogler, Reggie Schwarz and Aubrey Faulkner – took 106 wickets between them to secure series wins in 1905–06 (1–4) and 1909–10 (2–3). Gallingly, the London-born Schwarz had learned the tricks of the trade while playing with Bosanquet at Middlesex. Batsmen felt the delivery was a sleight of hand that had no place in what they fondly thought of as a morally transparent sport. In other words, they were angry because they had no idea how the hell they were going to pick it.

In his *Morning Post* article, entitled 'The Scapegoat of Cricket', Bosanquet explained his secrets. 'The googly . . . is nothing more or less than an ordinary off-break,' he wrote. 'The method of delivery is the secret of its difficulty, and this merely consisted in turning the WRIST over at the moment of delivery far enough to alter the axis of spin, so that a ball which normally delivered would break from leg, breaks from the off.'

Put simply, the googly is delivered from the back of the hand rather than from the side, and few leg-spinners have felt comfortable heading to work without it, even if Shane Warne uses it far less now than he used to. But how did it get its name? No one is quite sure, although one tempting argument has it that the Australians ensnared by Bosanquet were so mesmerized by the delivery that their eyes goggled. Its legacy lived on: in a letter to the *Observer* in January 2006, Mr Vernon Roper reminded everyone that 'in the 1930s a "googly ball" was a child's toy, shaped like a RUGBY ball with flattened ends, that bounced in unexpected directions and at random angles'.

Jack Iverson literally provided a twist when he learned how to deliver the googly from between his thumb and middle finger, and thus – unusually – out of the front of his hand. During the 1950–51 Ashes, at the age of thirty-five, he took 21 English wickets at an AVERAGE of 15 as Australia won 4–1. But he had a fragile temperament and chose never to play Test cricket again. In October 1973, following a period of depression, Iverson shot himself. His bowling methods were later imitated by his compatriot John Gleeson, who went on to take 93 wickets in 29 Tests. These days, the googly's spiritual home has shifted to Pakistan, where the baton has passed from Abdul Qadir via Mushtaq Ahmed to Danish Kaneria, whose googly is reckoned by Richie BENAUD, a former leg-spinner himself, to be the best in the world.

Famous googlies include the one sent down by England's Eric Hollies to bowl Don BRADMAN in his final Test innings in 1948, and Mushtaq's delivery in the 1992 World Cup final to trap Graeme Hick LEG BEFORE WICKET. Back in Bosanquet's day both Hollies and Mushtaq might have been accused of poor sportsmanship. 'If batsmen display a marked inability to hit the ball on the off-side or anywhere in front of the wicket and stand in apologetic attitudes before the wicket,' wrote the man himself, 'it is said that the googly has made it impossible for them to attempt the old aggressive attitude and make the scoring strokes.' But Bradman, who was denied a Test AVERAGE of 100, and Hick, who missed out on a World Cup winner's medal, both knew they had simply been outsmarted by one of the game's most ingenious inventions.

See also INVINCIBLES; MYSTERY.

GRACE, W. G. (1848–1915)

Whatever you think of William Gilbert Grace, the doctor from Bristol who – in the mock-epic language of his day – bestrode nineteenth-century cricket like a colossus, there is no escaping him and his ominous embonpoint. His beard is iconic, a facial adornment to rival the whiskers of Fidel Castro, Santa Claus and Noel Edmonds. And in 2005, Channel 4 used him – or rather they used a man with a pillow up his shirt – as the basis for their ASHES trailers. He was, as they say, a phenomenon. In fact, he still is.

As an ALL-ROUND cricketer and competitor he was light years ahead of his time. In a 43-year career for England, Gloucestershire and London County, Grace scored 54,896 runs, which places him fifth in the all-time list, and took 2,876 WICKETS, which places him sixth (though sources do disagree on the exact figures). He captained England against Australia in thirteen Tests, and won eight of them, including four series out of five, which is in itself enough to make him a national treasure. And he is widely credited as being the first player to develop a batting technique off both front and back foot, a skill today's generation practise in their sleep, or possibly on *Strictly Come Dancing*. Had he not died in 1915, there is every chance he would have co-signed the Treaty of Versailles and pipped Armstrong to the moon.

Yes, Grace was very much the father of the modern game, if not the godfather (in the style of Marlon Brando rather than the genial uncle who tells you not to spend it all at once). Because as well as being an imposing cricketer, WG was a master in the dark arts of gamesmanship. Tales of his rudeness abound. 'They've come to watch me bat, not you umpire,' he was supposed to have said in his high-pitched West Country voice after being bowled first ball in a charity match. And his reputation as a bit of a cad was summed up by the Essex fast bowler Charles Kortright. 'Surely you're not leaving us already, doctor,' he noted triumphantly after bowling Grace during a championship match in which he had been particularly reluctant to head to the pavilion. 'There's one stump still standing!'

Another story credits Grace, indirectly, with the birth

of the Ashes. When the young Australian batsman Sammy Jones left his CREASE to pat down a bump on the pitch during the Oval Test of 1882, Grace promptly ran him out. The Australian fast bowler Frederick 'The Demon' Spofforth later poked his luxuriantly moustachioed features round the door of the England dressing-room to let WG know that his gesture would 'cost you the match'. More than a century before Devon Malcolm was supposed to have informed South Africa's batsmen that 'You guys are history!', Spofforth charged in to take 7 for 44 and skittle England for 77 as they chased 85. *The Sporting Life* printed its famous mock obituary of English cricket, and the Ashes were born.

But perhaps the ultimate evidence that Grace deserved the label 'The Special One', years before the Chelsea manager Jose Mourinho applied it to himself, can be found in the 'Births and Deaths' section of WISDEN. Ostensibly a po-faced record of the lifespans of international cricketers, it included an entry for his mum, Martha, who is described as 'Mother and cricketing mentor of W. G.' She was even powerful enough to have brought to a halt a county championship match at which she was not actually present. When she died on 25 July 1884, the game between Lancashire and Gloucestershire was stopped because both WG and his elder brother EM (Edward Mills) were playing in it. Throughout his long career, the doctor never came up with a better excuse.

See also GOLDEN AGE; SLEDGING; WALKING.

GREENSWARD

The occasional tendency of cricket writing to lapse into the antediluvian is exemplified by greensward, which is a posh word for grass. The trouble is, once you've used the word, you are obliged to describe what happens on it by using one of the following verbs or verbal phrases: take to, do battle on, caper on, grace, or adorn. Greenswards are far too poetic simply to be 'played' on. Exploits take place on greenswards, full of derring-do and heroism. Matches always boil down to the last ball. Players become better people. Life is good. Except if, like the former West Indies batsman Lawrence Rowe, you were allergic to grass. 'Damnable greensward!' as Rowe almost certainly never said.

GRUBBER

A ball that hardly bounces after pitching, usually because it has hit either a crack or a loose piece of earth. Technically, the grubber – or mollygrubber, as Australians call it – is almost a no-ball (see law 24.6: 'Ball bouncing more than twice or rolling along the ground'), but usually it provides an opportunity for the aggrieved batsman, whose perfect forward defensive is only marginally less impressive than the sight of his off-stump cartwheeling behind him, to stare accusingly at the pitch and shake his head in the direction of the groundsman.

See also EXTRAS; UNDERARM BOWLING.

HAIR

In the old days it was simple. Hair was either what Denis Compton slapped Brylcreem on, or the thing which stood up on the back of an Englishman's neck when Don BRADMAN failed to score a double-century. Then Ian Botham and Jeff Thomson decided to grow old-rocker blond mullets, and cricket's relationship with hair was never the same again. Graham Gooch and Greg Matthews, the off-spinning Australian ALL-ROUNDER, both began sprouting new thatches after developing a timely arrangement with a company of hair-restorers, and they were joined in 2005 by Shane Warne, who denied he was balding but still took part in a gloriously awful TV ad with the now-hirsute Gooch. Jason Gillespie's curly mullet was entirely *au naturel*, but the same could not be said of the style preferred by Kevin Pietersen, who looked as if he had just had a disagreement with a jar of mustard. Botham, conveniently forgetting his own crimes against hairdressing, compared the look to a dead mongoose. But in the case of Sri Lanka's Sanath Jayasuriya, vanity proved costly. Bending down in the shower to pick up his shampoo, he slipped and dislocated a shoulder. Since he was practically bald anyway, he might have saved himself the bother.

HALF-VOLLEY

A ball that pitches invitingly close to the batsman, the half-volley is usually described as 'long' (it can hardly be short) or 'juicy', probably because it causes the batsman to salivate. In a metaphorical sense, if you are patting back a series of half-volleys, you might be taking part in a particularly banal radio interview – one in which neither interviewer nor interviewee wants to ruffle feathers. It can also be a term of abuse. An English cricket journalist, and part-time fast bowler, introduced his Labrador, Bumper, to colleagues in the press box. 'He's named after my favourite delivery!' he announced proudly. 'What, half-volley?' came the inevitable quip.

See also BOUNCER.

HAT-TRICK

Controversially, the origin of the term 'hat-trick' – three wickets in three successive balls by the same bowler – involves headwear. But the precise etymology is unclear. According to the *Oxford English Dictionary*, it came into use 'after H. H. Stephenson took three wickets in three balls for the all-England eleven against the twenty-two of Hallam at the Hyde Park ground, Sheffield in 1858.' The *OED* goes on: 'A collection was held for Stephenson (as was customary for outstanding feats by professionals) and he was presented with a cap or hat bought with the proceeds.' Other versions claim that successful bowlers were given a cap or hat for free; even that a collection would be taken among the crowd, who generously placed their florins and farthings in – you guessed it – a hat.

The Oxford Companion to Australian Cricket says the word was used in print for the first time in 1878, when Frederick Spofforth did the deed against eighteen of Hastings and District at The Oval. Spofforth was also the first bowler to take a hat-trick in a Test, when he removed Royle (bowled), MacKinnon (bowled) and Emmett (caught Horan) en route to match figures of 13 for 110 against England at Melbourne in January 1879. Since then, up to the end of January 2006, there have been a further thirty-five Test hat-tricks – a disproportionate seventeen of them since 1994 – including two on the same day by Australia's Jimmy Matthews against South Africa at Old Trafford during the first match of the 1912 Triangular Tournament.

Maurice Allom took a hat-trick, and four wickets in five balls, on his Test debut for England against New Zealand at Christchurch in January 1930, while Pakistan's Wasim Akram uniquely achieved the feat in successive matches against Sri Lanka during the Asian Test Championship in March 1999. In November that year at Harare, Sri Lanka's Nuwan Zoysa dismissed Zimbabwe's Trevor Gripper, Murray Goodwin and Neil Johnson with his first three balls of the match. Unfortunately for him, a power failure meant TV viewers missed the magic moment. Zoysa's opening partner in that game, Chaminda Vaas, would later become the first bowler to begin an international match with a hat-trick when he reduced Bangladesh to 0 for 3 at the start of a World Cup fixture at Pietermaritzburg in February 2003. And in January 2006, India's Irfan Pathan stunned Pakistan by removing Salman Butt, Younis Khan and Mohammad Yousuf with the last three balls of the first over of the third and deciding Test at Karachi. India still contrived to lose.

Hat-tricks can also be taken across two innings, two days,

or even two matches. But Jonathan Rice, in *Curiosities of Cricket*, mentions the feat of Jed Bowers of Trevose in Cornwall, who took three wickets in three balls spread over three seasons: 1989, '90 and '91. It is unknown whether he ever got the chance to make it four in four.

See also ASHES, THE.

HAWKEYE

A network of cameras, computers and 3-D images was never going to appeal to the old school, but Hawkeye has revolutionized the way lbws are perceived. Now, when the gnarled old-pro-turned-umpire informs the debutant SEAM bowler with no more than a tilt of the head that the ball was missing leg-stump, his supposedly intuitive under-standing of the game's geometry can be put to the test. Created by Paul Hawkins, a former Buckinghamshire cricketer with a Ph.D. in artificial intelligence, Hawkeye uses six cameras around the ground to help generate images of the flight of the ball, even if the flight is inter-rupted by a cynically positioned front pad. When Channel 4 first used the system to spice up their coverage in 2001, it became apparent that the umpires were getting a lot wrong – mainly because they were being over-generous to the batsmen. Traditionalists moaned that the machine's lack of human intelligence meant it was incapable of having a feel for the game, but this was romance for the sake of it. And if Hawkeye made the occasional error, then it was still an improvement on the inevitable mistakes made every game by the umpires.

See also ANALYST, THE; LEG BEFORE WICKET; SNICKOMETER.

HEAVY BALL

A fancy name for a delivery that is bowled with more oomph than usual. In theory, the heavy ball hits the bat harder than the batsman expected, and is thus a supposed shock tactic. In reality, the bowler just put in a little bit of extra effort, for which he is rewarded with a new piece of terminology. It's the sort of language that would have Fred Trueman spluttering into his pint of best.

HELMETS

In *The Art of Captaincy* Mike Brearley addresses the question of whether helmets are cowardly. 'The most obvious response is, what's so special about helmets? Is it unmanly to wear pads and gloves? And what about the BOX?' Brearley was writing in 1985, when – thanks in part to the strange-looking skullcap he began wearing in 1977 – helmets had only been in fashion for a few years. These days, they are taken for granted, except in the case of Viv Richards, a swaggering advert for alpha-maleness, who said he was 'always willing to back my GOD-given talents'.

The first example of protective headwear in cricket came in the 1870s, when Nottinghamshire's Richard Daft threw fashion to the wind by wrapping a towel round his head while batting on a treacherous pitch at LORD'S. Patsy Hendren, scorer of more FIRST-CLASS runs (57,611) than anyone bar Jack Hobbs (61,237) and Frank Woolley (58,969), was persuaded to experiment after being hit on the head in the Caribbean. In 1933, playing for Middlesex against West Indies, he wore what Geoffrey Moorhouse describes in his book *Lord's* as a cap with 'three peaks, two of them covering his ears and temples, lined with foam rubber; in appearance not at all unlike the thing Mike Brearley was to adopt forty-four years later'. To add an extra dimension to the jibes that Hendren undoubtedly had to put up with, the cap was made by his wife.

The Essex opener Dickie Dodds imaginatively wore part of a riding helmet under his cap in the 1950s, while Brearley began wearing his contraption in 1977. But protective headwear as we know it today did not take shape until Dennis Amiss wore what amounted to a crash helmet during Kerry PACKER's World Series Cricket. Designed by Vellvic, a company from Birmingham, it was made of fibreglass with a polycarbonate visor and could, in Amiss's words, 'take a double-barrel shotgun from 10 paces'.

The only problem was that the helmet covered his ears, which meant Amiss became involved in a series of run-outs as the habitual call of 'Yes . . . no . . . wait!' became 'Ehhhhh . . . ooooh . . . aaaahhh.' Today's models are far more ear-friendly, but you still have to ask why Alan Titchmarsh valued the Amiss original at only £300–500 for the BBC's *Antiques Roadshow* in 2005.

Amiss's enterprise impressed his fellow WSC rebels. After David Hookes was hit on the head by Andy Roberts in the Sydney Supertest in December 1977, Packer immediately ordered a batch of Vellvics from Birmingham to protect his players. Amiss, Tony Greig and Barry Richards were soon joined as helmet converts by Alan Knott, Zaheer Abbas, Mushtaq Ahmed, Rick McCosker and Ian Davis. And when Hookes returned to action following his tête-à-ball with Roberts, he wore one too. Vellvic was, says Gideon Haigh, 'a badge proclaiming World Series Cricket's "otherness"'.

The fashion spread. Australia's Graham Yallop became the first player to wear a helmet in a Test when he made

47 and 14 for Australia during a nine-wicket defeat by West Indies at Bridgetown in March 1978 (although England fans prefer to remember him as the man who captained a side weakened by Packer defections to a 5–1 ASHES defeat at home after he had light-heartedly predicted a 6–0 Australian win).

'I maintain that for most batsmen it's a good thing to be less cautious, but that the helmet does not make them rash,' argued Brearley, who claimed his career was 'rejuvenated by the assurance a helmet brings'. Ever the lateral-thinker (Brearley now practises psychoanalysis), he once placed a helmet at short midwicket during a county game between Middlesex and Yorkshire. The aim was to lure the batsman into a LEADING EDGE as he played against the spin of the slow left-armer Phil Edmonds in the hope of picking up the five runs that are available for hitting the helmet. But the authorities quickly put a stop to the tomfoolery: thereafter all unworn helmets had to be placed behind the wicketkeeper, which made sense – always assuming, of course, that your keeper could actually catch.

See also BOUNCER; DISMISSALS; FIELDING POSITIONS; MASTER, THE.

HOOK

The rebellious tearaway in cricket's school of strokeplay. The hook is a full-blooded, horizontal-batted bludgeon to the leg-side against a delivery that might have gone on to hit the head. The shot is full of risk because most of the time the ball goes in the air and there will be one or two men waiting on the BOUNDARY, desperate to make a fool of the batsman. Which is what makes the hook shot such a death-or-glory option. If it works, it looks great, infuriates the bowler and electrifies the crowd. If it fails, it looks awful and rumours begin to spread about the batsman's intellectual acuity. The crime is doubly bad if it is repeated by the captain, who at all times is unreasonably committed to set an example. When Ian Chappell kept getting out to the hook shot during the 1972 ASHES in England, he was startled to receive an aerogramme from his gran Dorothy. 'Dear, a lot of commentators are saying you should give up hooking,' she warned. 'Maybe you should consider it.'

See also DAVIS, GEORGE; PULL; SHOCKER.

HOWZAT

The most frequently asked question by bowlers, followed closely by 'You're joking, aren't you?' and 'How many fingers am I holding up?' Howzat is a contraction of the genteel 'How is that', which is how bowlers used to appeal for lbws and caught-behinds. Nowadays it sounds more like 'Howzeeeeee' or 'Haaaaaaaaaa'. The assumption is that these banshee-like wails are indeed appeals for a wicket, although they also sound like the kind of noise you might make if Inzamam-ul-Haq trod on your little toe, so nothing should be taken for granted. The best appeals involve all four limbs arranged in a star shape (see Richard Hadlee and Dominic Cork) and a primeval roar towards the heavens (see the entire Australian team). On such occasions it is easy to see why howzat tends to be regarded by the players as a statement rather than a question.

See also ALL-ROUNDER; LEG BEFORE WICKET.

HURRY-UP

A Trojan horse of a present from the bowler to the bats-man, usually in the form of a surprisingly fast ball. To give someone the hurry-up is to remind them not to take any liberties with your bowling. But if your hurry-up delivery is smacked for four, you know you're in trouble.

See also HEAVY BALL.

HYPEREXTENSION

If, in a strange parallel universe, Jennifer Aniston were hosting a cricket documentary, this is the moment she would say: 'Here comes the science bit. Concentrate.' L'Oréal hairspray, though, has nothing on hyperextension. For cricketing purposes, this occurs when the bowling arm straightens beyond the natural boundary of the elbow joint because of the speed at which the arm flies through the air. John Harmer, a biomechanics expert who has coached both the Australian and English WOMEN'S teams, has compared the effect to the bend that occurs in the shaft of a golf club on the downswing. To the naked eye it looks as if the bowler is CHUCKING. In fact, argues the defence, he is simply a victim of his own vigour.

Shoaib Akhtar, the man nicknamed the Rawalpindi Express and the first cricketer to touch 100mph in match conditions, is hyperextension's very own *cause célèbre*, and has twice been briefly banned because of his action. It was also queried as recently as February 2006, but the complaint needs to be put in context: it came from Greg Chappell, who had just coached India to a series defeat against Pakistan. Bruce Elliott, a biomechanics expert from Perth who regularly tests suspect actions, explained that 'Shoaib gets hyperextension, which the ICC says is OK, and rightly so. Otherwise, you would run into problems with disability and people would take them to the high court.' Elliott believes Shoaib is double-jointed.

.

ICC (INTERNATIONAL CRICKET COUNCIL)

The International Cricket Council's mission statement declares that it will 'lead by promoting the game as a global sport, protecting the spirit of cricket and optimizing commercial opportunities for the benefit of the game'. Some feel it would have been better off sorting out the mess which eventually led to Zimbabwe suspending their own Test status in January 2006, instead of organizing little-loved tournaments in the name of 'optimizing commercial interests', but governing bodies rarely please all of the people all the time. Its critics feel the ICC fails to please any of the people any of the time, and when the Council stepped in to warn the Australians and South Africans not to say nasty things about each other ahead of their Test series in 2005–06, the former Australia fast bowler Jeff Thomson described the organization as 'a waste of space'.

The ICC began life in 1909 as the Imperial Cricket Conference after representatives from England, Australia and South Africa met at LORD'S. They were joined in 1926 by India, New Zealand and West Indies; in 1953 by Pakistan; in 1981 by Sri Lanka; in 1992 by Zimbabwe; and in 2000 by Bangladesh. South Africa left in 1961 and rejoined in 1991. In 1965 – and not before time – 'Imperial' changed to 'International' because non-Commonwealth nations were now allowed to join, and in 1989 'Conference' became 'Council', in order to reflect the more formal nature of the organization. Aside from the ten full members, there are thirty-two Associate members, from the Cayman Islands to the USA, and fifty-six Affiliate members, from Guernsey to Iran.

In 2005 the ICC moved from its headquarters at Lord's to Dubai on the Arabian peninsula for tax reasons. But observers also noted perspicaciously that Dubai was a lot closer to the subcontinent than it was to north London, and wondered whether the move was symptomatic of cricket's great power shift from the Anglo-Australians to the Asians. The cricketers just got on with playing the game, and occasionally complaining that the ICC Champions Trophy, played every two years in between World Cup cycles, was too much like hard work.

See also SLEDGING.

INITIALS

When Margaret Thatcher told *Woman's Own* magazine in 1987 that there was no such thing as society, a whole generation of so-called amateur cricketers must have choked on their caviar. Until 1963 the English game was divided between Gentlemen (amateurs, often of the amateur-only-for-the-purposes-of-the-taxman variety) and Players (the professionals for whom line and length meant tomorrow evening's fish and chips). It was a social apartheid that still affects the way people view the sport today. The division was at its most obvious in the pavilion, where the two groups used different dressing-rooms. But it also flexed its rabble-suppressing muscles on match scorecards.

Amateurs were indicated by initials which preceded the surname; professionals by initials which followed it. When the Middlesex pro Fred Titmus was wrongly referred to as 'F. J. Titmus' on one scorecard, the LORD's announcer nipped a potential armed rebellion in the bud by telling spectators that the entry should in fact have read 'Titmus, F. J.' Embarrassed glances were exchanged and old school ties adjusted.

In the days when these things apparently mattered, multiple initials stood you in good stead. J. W. H. T. Douglas (who won a boxing gold at middleweight at the 1908 Olympics), A. P. F. Chapman, R. E. S. Wyatt, G. O. B. Allen, N. W. D. Yardley and P. B. H. May all captained England between 1921 and 1956, since when the only three-initialled skippers have been M. J. K. Smith, the anything-but-plummy K. W. R. Fletcher and R. G. D. Willis (who added the 'D' himself in honour of Bob Dylan). Of the first six, only Yardley (a Yorkshireman who went to Cambridge) came from the north. Either side of the Pennines, the tendency has been to avoid the frivolity of middle names altogether. W. Rhodes, H. Sutcliffe, C. Washbrook, L. Hutton, D. Gough and A. Flintoff all hail from Yorkshire or Lancashire, and would probably greet the concept of an extra name with a contemptuous snort.

Sonny Ramadhin, whose mixture of offies and leggies propelled West Indies to their first Test win at Lord's in 1950, did not even have the luxury of a single initial when he left Trinidad for the England tour that summer. He used 'Sonny' because that's what his friends at school called him, 'but when I got to England they insisted that nobody could go through life without initials', he told Peter Johnson of the *Daily Mail* almost half a century later. 'The next time I picked up the paper I'd become "K. T. Ramadhin". I never did find out what my new English names were supposed to be.'

Nowadays, the Sri Lankans are helping the initial to launch a spirited comeback. The left-arm seamer W. P. U. J. C. Vaas holds the record among contemporary international cricketers, but his five-letter salute is swamped by compatriot A. R. R. A. P. W. R. R. K. B. Amunugama. In the 2004 edition of *WISDEN*, which records Amunugama's feats for Antonians, the editor, Matthew Engel, assures us that the initials stand for Amunugama Rajapakse Rajakaruna Abeykoon Panditha Wasalamudiyanse Ralahamilage Rajitha Krishantha Bandara Amunugama – or Ranjith for short. Yet despite the best efforts of Ranjith's mum and dad, the selectors stubbornly refuse to offer him the Sri Lankan captaincy.

See also JOURNALISM; WALKING.

INNINGS

A simple enough concept referring either to the collective effort of the batsmen ('England were all out for 46 in their second innings') or the contribution of each individual ('Alec Stewart top-scored with a plucky innings of 18'). The matter is sometimes complicated by irresponsible tea-towels sold in Cotswold villages to unsuspecting tourists containing gems along the lines of 'When the team that is out comes in, the team that has been in goes out, until they are out, at which point they go back in.' If nothing else, these convolutions help convince the English that their sport is beyond the comprehension of mere continental Europeans, Americans and Japanese.

See also FRENCH CRICKET; USA.

INVINCIBLES

It's one of cricket's fondest imponderables: which was the greatest Test team of them all? The short-list usually boils down to three: Clive Lloyd's 1980s West Indians, Steve Waugh's turn-of-the-millennium Australians, and Don BRADMAN's Invincibles, the immodest but accurate name given to the Australia side which toured England in the summer of 1948. Not only did they whip the hosts 4–0 – still England's worst defeat in a home ASHES series – but they went through the entire tour without losing a match, a feat achieved by no Australian side before or since.

In all, they played 31 games and won 23, a staggering 15 of those by an innings. They AVERAGED a colossal 50 runs per wicket, against a feeble 19 by the opposition. They hit a combined total of 47 hundreds and conceded only 7. Even when you consider Jack Fingleton's assessment, in his seminal book on the tour, *Brightly Fades the Don*, that 'the English team of 1948 was the poorest that had played against Australia in the twentieth century', these are a phenomenal set of statistics. From April to September, the likes of Bradman, Keith Miller, Ray Lindwall, Arthur Morris, Sid Barnes and Neil Harvey did pretty well as they pleased, which included scoring 721 in a day against Essex. They might even have been a match for an all-time World XI.

But this was also a tour about one man. At the age of thirty-nine and with his health the subject of concern,

Bradman knew he was on his last legs. From the moment his arrival on board the RMS *Strathaird* in Fremantle, Perth, on 18 March was greeted with a cry of 'He's on!' he was the glint in the jewel in the centre of the crown. He began with a gentle 107 in the win at Worcester and finished with a knock of 153 at Scarborough against H. D. G. Leveson-Gower's XI, when he ran off the field without bothering to check whether Len Hutton had completed the catch that would end his last innings in England. In between he summoned the energy and the genius to hit an unbeaten 173 to help Australia chase down over 400 to win the fourth Test at Headingley, a ground where he averaged 192 against England; and he made an immortal DUCK in what turned out to be his final Test innings, at The Oval. Had England's batsmen not capitulated so pathetically in that match, he might have had a second innings in which to score either the 4 not out or the 104 he needed to finish with a Test average of 100. It was not to be.

Fingleton recalls the build-up to Bradman's Oval farewell. 'Hundreds in this crowd had queued all night. They had slept on wet pavements so that they could see this final Test and the final appearance of Bradman, and his reception could not have been bettered. He came a lithe, athletic figure down the steps, and he fingered his cap to the applause as he made his way to the middle, his trunk slightly bent forward off his legs.

'The reception he received must have been embarrassing for him. It lasted all the way to the middle, and there Yardley [the England captain] had assembled his team and called for three cheers for Bradman. This the English team gave heartily and Yardley shook Bradman by the hand. Bradman took guard, looked about and settled himself.

Hollies bowled him a good one which Bradman played off the back foot. The next was pitched slightly farther up. It drew Bradman forward, he missed and the ball crashed into his stumps. And what a roar there was from the crowd!'

For a moment, Bradman was not invincible. But then not even the best offerings ever do exactly what they say on the tin.

See also CHARACTER; GOOGLY; INITIALS.

JAFFA

An unplayable ball. Of course, the word unplayable is one of those sporting expressions that is used more often than it should be, like 'catastrophe', 'incredible', and 'Sue Barker'. But it helps convey a sense that each day of sport is more exciting than the last, and is thus a favourite with commentators and journalists, who have a vested interest in making the public believe that this really is the case. Jaffa is an ancient city in Israel which grows the large, oval-shaped oranges whose juiciness might help explain why mouth-watering deliveries are so-called. The reference is lost on the locals.

JOURNALISM

Cricket-writing has come a long way since the days when match reports habitually began by telling readers who won the TOSS and whether the sun was shining (usually Australia, and, no, it wasn't). Then along came Neville Cardus, who in the 1920s began to use the generous space he received in the *Manchester Guardian* to paint verbal pictures which were more akin to impressionism than realism. If the actual events fitted in with the way Cardus saw them, so much the better. But Cardus, who preferred to associate himself with his other job – as a music critic – had paved the way for a more whimsical style of journalism that would later find echo in the writings of R. C. Robertson-Glasgow, Alan Ross and Matthew Engel.

But, as Engel himself wrote in *Wisden Cricket Monthly* in April 2000, Cardus was only one of two schools of English cricket-writing in the twentieth century. The other was spawned by E. W. 'Jim' Swanton, who emerged from his war-time tribulations in Burma to become the cricket correspondent of the *Daily Telegraph*, a paper which provided a natural home for his stentorian pronouncements until shortly before his death in 2000. Natural successors include John Woodcock and Christopher Martin-Jenkins. If Swanton represented the establishment, Cardus was the impish outsider. 'His writing was rare entertainment,' wrote Swanton in 1999, 'based on the complete reversal of the aphorism "Comment is free, fact is sacred".' It was almost certainly intended with affection.

These days the must-reads in the press box include Scyld Berry of the *Sunday Telegraph*, the Melbourne-based free-lance Gideon Haigh, the Pom-turned-Cobber Peter Roebuck, and Rahul Bhattacharya from Mumbai. C. L. R. James was more of a historian than a journalist, but very few books have ever placed sport in their social context as vividly as *Beyond a Boundary*, his tale of the Caribbean's coming-of-age.

See also DOT BALLS; PRESS CONFERENCE; WISDEN; WS, THE THREE.

JOYRIDING

The handbrake turn might sound like one of Muttiah Muralitharan's more obscure variations, but cricket and joyriding did once come into close contact, however tenuously. The RAIN-ruined draw between Essex and Surrey at Valentines Park in Ilford in June 2001 was enlivened when a joyrider escaped through the park after crashing his car nearby. It was thought that his dash for freedom was the last throw of the fluffy dice.

KOLPAK

The sport of handball gets as much publicity in the cricket-playing nations as Graeco-Roman wrestling and pelota. Handball goalkeepers get even less, unless commentators are referring ad nauseam to the former Manchester United keeper Peter Schmeichel's schoolboy days in Denmark, which he seemed to spend 'making himself big' in the handball goal. But in 2003, a Slovakian handball goalie playing for Östringen in the second division of the German league changed all that, and in the process introduced a new insult into the county game.

That year Maros Kolpak – the surname is best pronounced with a disdainful curl of the lip – took the Deutscher Handball-Bund (the German handball federation) to the European Court over their decision to classify him as a foreigner. The court ruled that because Slovakia had a trade agreement with countries in the European Union (it would not actually join the EU until May 2004), Kolpak could play as a local, a decision which in effect lifted all restrictions on the number of non-Germans playing in the German leagues.

The repercussions for cricket were immediate: players from nations which had a similar trade agreement – such as South Africa, Zimbabwe and many of the Caribbean islands – could now play county cricket without being classed as overseas players (a quaint cricketism that harks unconsciously back to the days when Britannia ruled the waves). In theory, county teams which had previously been limited to a maximum of two imports per match did not now need to field any English-born cricketers at all. Cricket-lovers grumbled disconsolately about the end of the world as they knew it, and began to compare Kolpak with Beelzebub himself. Over in Östringen, Kolpak laughed with delight when he was told that his name was being taken in vain in the press-boxes of Worcester and Derby. At the age of thirty-two he was proving that a life-time of having a hard ball hurled at you from 10 metres away need not render the glass half empty.

Stories about hordes of Kolpak cricketers marching north through Africa or sailing across the Atlantic from the West Indies in the dead of night spread round the county circuit. Cricketers' children were sent to bed early and street lights turned off. But with the exception of poorly supported clubs like Leicestershire and Northamptonshire – Kolpakshire to their critics – the invasion never really happened. This was mainly because the ECB introduced an incentivization scheme whereby counties would receive financial reward for producing England-qualified players. It left Maros Kolpak's hopes of opening the batting against Australia at LORD's dangling by a thread. But his fame had already been assured. And so too his infamy.

KWIK CRICKET

An innovative ECB brainchild aimed at introducing youngsters to cricket and spelling.

LAST-CHANCE SALOON

Favoured drinking haunt of cricketers who are one failure away from being dropped for good. Graeme Hick and Mark Ramprakash spent most of their international careers supping nervously here, while Phil DeFreitas, who was ditched on a record thirteen separate occasions by the England selectors, was regularly asked to leave at closing time, only to be invited back when the doors opened at noon the next day. No wonder he always looked confused when he ran in to bowl.

See also BOUNCER; FLAT-TRACK BULLY.

LEADING EDGE

What batsmen risk getting if they are aiming to the legside and play their shot too early. The leading edge is the outside portion of the bat and it can make a batsman look very silly indeed: instead of the ball disappearing through midwicket, it loops in a gentle curve to the man at cover. Cameramen can be fooled too, and will often follow the non-existent path of the ball to the leg-side fence while viewers wonder why the fielders are hugging and high-fiving.

See also FIELDING POSITIONS.

LEARNING CURVE

Always steep.

LEG BEFORE WICKET

Lbw is to cricket what the off-side rule is to FOOTBALL: it is always the first thing people point to when they say they don't understand the game. There is no excuse for this. Put simply, if the ball hits a part of the batsman other than his bat (or the gloves as long as they are holding the bat), did not pitch outside leg-stump, and would in the opinion of the umpire have gone on to hit the wicket, then the batsman is out leg-before. Complications arise when you delve into the detail – and the history of the development of the lbw law is almost worth a book in itself – but we're not talking Fermat's Last Theorem here. If the batsman is hit outside the line of off-stump and is playing a shot, then he is not out. If he is playing no shot – this is usually obvious – then his fate is in the hands of the umpire. And that, ladies and gentlemen, is that.

See also SHOULDER ARMS.

LEG-BREAK

If OFF-BREAKS are the meat and two veg of the slow-bowling menu, leg-breaks are the bacon-and-egg ice cream, since they have the potential to be either sensational or awful. Delivered out of the side of the right hand with a flick of the WRIST, the leg-break TURNS from leg to off, but is much harder to control than its sturdier, more reliable off-break cousin. Until Shane Warne stunned Mike Gatting in 1993, leg-spin was regarded as a throwback to more innocent times. Suddenly, it became fashionable again, except in England, where – with apologies to Ian Salisbury and Chris Schofield – the last international class leg-spinner was Doug Wright, who retired in 1957.

See also MYSTERY; WONDERBALL.

LIGHT METERS

Nothing is more guaranteed to provoke boos from the crowd than the sight of the umpires reaching into their pockets for their harbingers of doom, sorry, light meters. Readings are often taken at both ends of the pitch, which means that if one of the umpires is Steve Bucknor, who has never knowingly rushed from A to B, then it's practically game over anyway: by the time he has ambled the 22 yards the sun will already be a distant memory. Every time batsmen accept the offer of bad light, there's gnashing of teeth and wailing as if the extra two overs that might have been possible had they stayed on would have sent the crowd home delirious rather than suicidal. But then only two men have to face Wasim Akram and Waqar Younis in the gathering GLOOM, and it isn't the pair of drunks in Row F.

LOLLIPOP

A gift of a delivery which only the most incompetent batsman would fail to hit to the BOUNDARY. Despite the fact that lollipop is a singular noun, you often hear it with a plural verb ('That were a real lollipop'), mainly because the only person who uses the phrase is Geoff Boycott.

See also CORRIDOR OF UNCERTAINTY; STONEWALL.

LONG-HOP

If backbench MPs are frustrated cabinet ministers, and personal trainers are wannabe Olympic gymnasts, then the long-hop is little more than a failed BOUNCER. Insofar as both the long-hop and the bouncer land roughly halfway down the pitch, the distinction is a fine one. But the results are like chalk and cheese. Whereas the bouncer conveys menace, instils fear and breaks bones, the long-hop invites ridicule, sits up like a tennis ball and begs to be battered through midwicket. If we are honest, the distinction is often made once the batsman has played his stroke, at which point the armchair expert will begin to pontificate. 'Superb bouncer/rank long-hop,' he will say in quick succession about two almost identical balls. In truth, one batsman's bouncer is another's long-hop. It's just that the one who made it look like a long-hop is almost certainly the better player.

See also FULL-TOSS; HALF-VOLLEY.

LONG ROOM

The most evocative four walls in world cricket. The Long Room (note the capital letters: this is a place with a highly cultivated sense of its own importance) is the imposing chamber through which the players have to walk on their way to the middle at LORD'S. If they happen to be

Australian batsmen, they will generally be sent on their way with witticisms from MCC members like 'See you soon', which doesn't seem to bother them too much: the Australia opener Justin Langer has described walking through the Long Room as 'like being bearhugged by an invisible spirit'. In any case Australia lost only one Test at Lord's in the whole of the twentieth century.

The Long Room can feel a bit like a museum, with its collection of bats, balls, paintings and unfeasibly old men. The West Indies opener Jeff Stollmeyer said it was a room 'through which one felt one ought to tiptoe'. The former England captain Tony Lewis wrote that the 'players' NERVOUS walk out to bat, down the stairs and through the Long Room made me feel like an errand boy who had wandered by mistake into a club reading room and could not wait to get out the other end'. Presumably, though, he did not feel as nervous as the Northamptonshire captain Allan Lamb, who was accompanied through the Long Room on his way out to bat during the 1992 NatWest Trophy final win over Leicestershire to prevent anyone from handing him another writ. His former county colleague Sarfraz Nawaz had already delivered one before the start of the game over a piece Lamb had written in the *Daily Mirror* about BALL-TAMPERING.

But there have been enough moments to lighten the mood. On his Test debut in 1975, the England batsman David Steele – grey-HAIRED, bespectacled, 'like a bank clerk going to war' wrote one correspondent – got lost on his way out to bat and ended up in the pavilion's basement toilets. He recovered to score 50 and 45 and eventually win the BBC Sports Personality of the Year award.

Frank Keating recalls E. W. Swanton – a human embodiment of the Long Room, if ever there was one –

about to be interviewed in 1964 for a TV series called *Spring Out!* Seconds before the first question, his interviewer offered Swanton his mascara. 'And in the Long Room, too,' roared Keating. 'Mascara! Never can a gaze have been so malevolently withering, sustained and excruciatingly anguished. The interview was conducted as if EWS was squatting on a cactus.'

See also JOURNALISM.

LORD'S

It is the done thing when talking about Lord's to use one of the following phrases: 'HQ', 'the home of cricket', 'hallowed turf', 'unique atmosphere'. But not everyone has toed the line upon visiting St John's Wood in north London for the first time. Sunil Gavaskar was said to be unimpressed with the slope that runs from the Grandstand to the Tavern Stand, while Keith Miller, the post-war Australia ALL-ROUNDER who never minced his words, reckoned it was 'a crummy little ground'. He later changed his mind, and – on a sunny day, with England playing in front of a packed house of 30,000 – it's not hard to see why.

The apostrophe refers to the fact that the ground was bought by Thomas Lord, a Yorkshire-born bowler with the White Conduit Cricket Club in Islington. Irked by the tendency of *hoi polloi* to watch their matches, and keen to be closer to the gentlemen's clubs of central London, the aristocrats who whiled away their leisure time playing for White Conduit asked the entrepreneurial Lord to find them another venue. He came up with Dorset Fields in Marylebone (hence the MCC, or Marylebone Cricket

Club, founded – we can safely assume – in 1787), only to be forced out in 1811 by rising rental costs. But a year later Lord learned that his new ground in Marylebone Park was bang in the middle of Parliament's plans for the Regent Canal. And so Lord's moved to St John's Wood in 1814, to the site of a former DUCK pond, where it has stayed ever since. In 1825, Lord sold the ground to William Ward for £5,000.

Since then Lord's has become synonymous with the game in the same way that Wembley meant FOOTBALL and the Circus Tavern in Purfleet has become synonymous with darts. Middlesex were invited to play their home games there in 1877, and the ground staged the first three World Cup finals, in 1975, 1979 and 1983. Touring teams claim to be inspired by the surroundings, although only Australia (with fourteen wins to five defeats, only one of them in the twentieth century) have outplayed England regularly. Lord's still drips with history, but the media centre erected at the Nursery End has lent a huge dollop of space-aged modernity.

See also ASHES, THE; JOURNALISM; LONG ROOM; PRESS CONFERENCE; STONEWALL.

LUNCH

For many, the best bit of the day. The forty-minute lunch break – 'luncheon interval' at the posher venues – is both a glorious anachronism and a welcome opportunity for players, spectators and journalists to consider the relative merits of the bacon-and-brie panini or the chicken-and-avocado salad. Followers of other sports scoff at this ritual, but the sad truth is they are simply jealous, which is understandable when your best hope for a feed involves a fifteen-minute queue for a pie filled with industrial sludge.

The quality of most cricket lunches is the reason why no newspaper report ever contains details of the play that takes place between 12.45 and 1pm. Journalists are too busy bagging the best spot in the press-box queue, a fearsome institution which provides a neat twist to Darwin's theory of evolution: survival of the fattest. Most of them will then spend the twenty minutes after lunch asleep, dribbling happily into their laptops. This is the moment for less comatose members of the fourth estate to get their exclusives.

Traditionally, the best lunches on the circuit have been provided by LORD'S. Mike Selvey, the former Middlesex and England bowler who later became cricket correspondent of the *Guardian*, remembers the meals provided by Nancy Doyle, a sharp-tongued Irish lady who ruled the kitchen with an iron egg-whisk: 'No starters, but main courses you would want your mum to cook (sensational steak and kidney pie), heaps of vegetables, proper puddings and a cheese board to die for.' Selvey continues: 'Once Mike Brearley, captain of England, thought the soporific post-prandial mob he was leading perhaps needed less indulgence. Something a little less substantial, Nancy? "Tell you what, Michael," she countered, hands on hips. "I won't tell you how to fockin' bat and you don't tell me how to fockin' cook. All right?"'

Back in the days when Don BRADMAN would be served mid-session drinks in the outfield by two waitresses in starched aprons and a waiter in a bow-tie, lunches were more formal affairs, with both sets of players wearing their team blazers and shovelling in as much roast beef and potatoes as was humanly possible. Nowadays, the *specialité du jour* is more likely to be Carbohydrate Surprise or Protein Delight.

But Mark Butcher had a different recipe for success. After hitting an unbeaten 173 to win the Headingley Test against Australia in 2001, he revealed his method of recharging his batteries during the lunch break. 'I just sat in the shower and had a coffee and couple of cigarettes,' he said, in an instant undoing years of sterling work by the anti-smoking lobby.

LORD'S
MUSEUM

ORIGINAL
'BOWLED MAIDEN OVER'
JOKE

MAIDEN

An over in which no runs are scored (wides and no-balls preclude a maiden; byes and leg-byes do not). Also the basis of one of cricket's oldest and unfunniest gags: if you've never heard the one about bowling a maiden over, you haven't missed out. Garry Sobers once called for the abolition of maidens on the grounds that they encourage negative cricket, but if Sobers had had his cavalier way we would not be able to rejoice in statistics like this: the most maidens bowled in succession in a Test by one man is twenty-one, by India's notoriously stingy left-arm spinner Bapu Nadkarni against England at Madras (now Chennai) in January 1964. Nadkarni, who used to hone his trademark accuracy by aiming at a coin placed on a good length, returned figures of 32-27-5-0. In other words, if he had bowled from both ends for an entire day, the England batsmen would have been lucky to score 15. During the course of that five-Test series, he sent down 212 six-ball overs and conceded only 278 runs. It comes as no great surprise to learn that India and England drew 0–0.

See also DOT BALLS; EXTRAS; WOMEN.

MANHATTAN

A bar-graph detailing runs per over – and one of cricket's more tenuous links with the USA. On a good day for the batsmen, the graph will resemble the Manhattan skyline; on a bad day it will look more like the Fens. Either way, commentators usually spoil the graph by scribbling all over it with their fancy pens.

MANKAD

Mulvantrai Himmatlal Mankad – Vinoo, if we're being picky – was India's star ALL-ROUNDER in the years immediately after the Second World War. He once put on a world-record 413 with Pankaj Roy for the first wicket against New Zealand, and famously made 72 and 184, as well as bowling 73 overs in an innings, in a losing cause at LORD'S. But that is not why his surname gets a category of its own. Oh no. Because when India toured Australia in 1947–48, he gave his name to a type of DISMISSAL that is unlikely to have pride of place on the Mankad mantelpiece.

During a warm-up game against an Australian XI at Sydney, Mankad warned Bill Brown not to back up too far (leaving the CREASE at the non-striker's end before the ball has been bowled). Brown ignored him – and shortly afterwards lost his wicket when Mankad, bowling his slow left-armers, whipped off the bails in the act of pretending to deliver the ball. But the phrase 'to be Mankaded' only stuck after a repetition of the incident in a Test match at the same venue a month later, when Brown was run out for 18. 'When the umpire gave him out,' wrote a local journalist called 'Ginty' Lush, 'Brown raised his arm and swung it through the air in disgust.'

Years later, Courtney Walsh was praised for refusing to Mankad the Pakistan No. 11 Salim Jaffer during the 1987 World Cup. Thanks to Walsh's generosity, Pakistan won by one wicket off the last ball of the match and went on to qualify for the semi-finals ahead of West Indies. Walsh's only consolation was to receive a carpet from a grateful business in Karachi. To the consternation of potential Mankads everywhere, law 42.15 now states that a bowler cannot run out a batsman once he has entered his delivery stride.

MASTER, THE

An epithet that has passed from the England and Surrey batsman Jack Hobbs to Hanif Mohammad, then on to Sunil Gavaskar and finally to Sachin Tendulkar, although in the case of the diminutive Hanif, Gavaskar and Tendulkar, the term was cunningly prefaced by the word 'Little'. Hobbs was a force of nature, scoring a world-record 61,237 first-class runs and playing on past the age of fifty. Had it not been for the First World War, he would have become the only man to score 200 centuries, but instead he had to settle for 197, more than half of which came after he had turned forty. In March 1929 he hit a Test hundred at Melbourne at the age of forty-six – no one older has achieved the feat, and nor are they ever likely to. Encouragingly for duffers everywhere, he was self-taught, which makes his twelve ASHES hundreds – a record by an Englishman – all the more astonishing.

Hanif's fame usually rests on two innings: his 337 in over sixteen hours to defy West Indies at Bridgetown in January 1958, and his 499 (run out) for Karachi soon after. But he also deserves credit for turning cricket in Pakistan from a pastime for the elite into the people's game. He could keep wicket too, bowl with both arms, and run on one leg. Well, maybe not that last bit.

Gavaskar arrived on the scene with 774 runs at 154 in his first Test series, in the West Indies, and never really looked back, except when he tried to persuade his opening partner Chetan Chauhan to leave the field with him after receiving what he believed to be a poor lbw decision against Dennis Lillee at Melbourne in February 1981. Gavaskar's gift to India went beyond mere runs, although he made over 10,000 of them in Tests. In the words of Sambit Bal, the editor of CRICINFO magazine, he 'earned respect for Indian cricket and he taught his team-mates the virtue of professionalism. The self-actualisation of Indian cricket began under him.'

Tendulkar was his spiritual successor, a player so prodigious that when Don BRADMAN first saw him bat on TV he called his wife Jessie over and modestly croaked: 'Doesn't he remind you of me?' On 10 December 2005 he scored his thirty-fifth Test hundred, against Sri Lanka at Delhi, to pass Gavaskar's record. And when he hit his thirty-ninth one-day international century, against Pakistan at Peshawar two months later, he became the first player to pass 14,000 ODI runs. Perhaps no other sportsman in history has had so many adoring fans.

See also DISMISSALS; REARGUARD; STONEWALL.

MATCH-FIXING

The idea that gambling did not wrap its grubby tentacles around cricket's virgin goodness until Hansie Cronje came along is a complete fallacy, since WISDEN cites a 'wagger' (wager) of two shillings and sixpence on a match at Lewes in East Sussex in 1694. Without betting and match-fixing in the eighteenth century, matches might not even have taken place. But in the modern era it was not until Delhi police intercepted telephone calls implicating Cronje in a wide-reaching cash-for-information scandal that all hell broke loose. At first the news that one of the world's most famously Christian sportsmen had sold his soul to the bookies was greeted with disbelief. It was, wrote Tim de Lisle, as if the QUEEN had been caught fiddling her expenses. But after an initial denial, Cronje confessed and revelations began to emerge from all over the cricketing world. Some wondered whether they could ever trust the game again. Others, even more miserably, prepared for a life of following FOOTBALL.

There had already been suggestions that all was not as above board as it should be. Shane Warne, Mark Waugh and Tim May had claimed that during Australia's trip to Pakistan in late 1994 they were offered money by Salim Malik to underperform. Several years later Malik was banned for life, while Warne and Waugh were forced to admit that they had accepted payments from a biblical-sounding character known as John the bookmaker in return for information about weather, pitch conditions and team selection – a fact which was covered up by the Australian Cricket Board.

Two weeks before Cronje faced a South African judicial commission headed by Edwin King, a retired judge, Justice Qayyum published his report into match-fixing in Pakistan. Ata-ur-Rehman, a scapegoat in the eyes of many, was banned for life along with Malik, while several big names – including Wasim Akram, Waqar Younis and Inzamam-ul-Haq – were slapped over the wrists for what Qayyum called 'partial amnesia'. In 2006, Qayyum told CRICINFO that he had gone easy on Wasim because he had not wanted to see such a great cricketer dragged through the mud.

But it was the King Commission, which sat at Cape Town in June 2000, which really stole the show. Cronje admitted accepting payments of around $140,000 between 1996 and 2000 from an Indian bookie called Mukesh Gupta, but denied fixing a match. The closest he came was the Centurion Test against England in January 2000, which was saved from a watery draw when Cronje agreed with a local bookie called Marlon Aronstam to set up a run-chase for England in return for hard cash and a leather jacket.

Later that year, India's Central Bureau of Investigation revealed the findings of its own inquiry. The former India captain Mohammad Azharuddin was banned for life along with Ajay Sharma, while Ajay Jadeja and Manoj Prabhakar were banned for five years each. But virtually none of the main cricketing nations remained untouched: Gupta claimed to have had dealings with Martin Crowe (New Zealand), Aravinda de Silva (Sri Lanka), Brian Lara (West Indies) and Alec Stewart (England). None of the allegations was proved.

These days the players are kept on a tight rein by the ICC's Anti-Corruption Unit, but it has not stopped the whispers, even retrospectively. Was Bangladesh's win over Pakistan in the 1999 World Cup, a result which hastened their elevation to Test status, the result of sharp practice? Many prominent cricketing figures believed so. But then, post-Cronje, it was possible to believe anything.

See also DECLARATIONS; GOD.

MCC (MARYLEBONE CRICKET CLUB)

The MCC was founded in 1787, two years before the start of the French Revolution, although it's likely Marie-Antoinette would have received just as frosty a reception in London. WOMEN were not allowed to join this private club until 1998, by which time the MCC had, in the mind of the public, become synonymous with gin-soaked colonels peering through their monocles and reminiscing about the Charge of the Light Brigade. But this stereotype overlooks the work carried out by the MCC in spreading cricket's gospel around the world. England touring teams played under its banner until 1976–77, and until 1993, when the ICC assumed governance of the global game, M, C and C were the three most important INITIALS in cricket. The club still owns the copyright to the game's Laws. And, of course, it owns LORD'S, which has been the Club's home since 1814.

Membership remains so highly prized that it can take up to eighteen years to join, unless you cheat and score lots of runs for England first. This explains the sea of white HAIR that populates the pavilion during Test matches, when members would not be seen dead wearing anything but the club's bacon-and-egg tie. In fact, the sense of decorum is such that some members would not be seen dead being, well, dead. Jonathan Rice tells the story of the MCC member who passed away in his seat in the pavilion balcony shortly after TEA at a Test match in the early 1980s. To prevent alarm, a member of the groundstaff was given the task of sitting next to the ex-member and pretending to engage in a two-way chat with him for the whole of the final session. The suggestion that this was one of the more animated conversations overheard at Lord's is wholly without foundation.

METRONOME

In music, a metronome is a little machine that keeps time with a regular tick. In cricket, it is a bowler who maintains an automaton-like accuracy over after over, and is thus anything but music to the batsmen's ears. The player most frequently called metronomic is Australia's Glenn McGrath, who regularly returns figures of 25-13-39-3 and generally mesmerizes the opposition batsmen into submission. Just ask the former England captain Mike Atherton. In seventeen ASHES Tests, McGrath dismissed Atherton nineteen times, which was one more than the previous world record between two players (England's Alec Bedser to Australia's Arthur Morris). McGrath's consistent line and length are reflected by the fact that Atherton was caught behind ten times and caught by other fielders – mainly in the slips – on eight occasions. In fact, Atherton made something of a habit of being transfixed by familiar faces: the two West Indian greats Curtly Ambrose and Courtney Walsh both claimed his wicket seventeen times in Tests. Still, at least he was consistent.

MICHELLE

Bear with us on this one. When a bowler picks up five wickets in an innings, he has taken what is often known as a five-for. Stress the first syllable and it sounds vaguely like (Michelle) Pfeiffer, the Hollywood actress who starred in *The Witches of Eastwick*, *Dangerous Liaisons* and *The Fabulous Baker Boys*. The fact that she now gets a mention umpteen times a season in county dressing-rooms from Cardiff to Canterbury possibly ranks less highly on her CV.

See also BUNSEN.

MILITARY MEDIUM

Praise can come no fainter. To be designated as medium-pace is hard enough for a bowler who has always imagined himself to be 'fast'. But to have 'military' stuck on the front is beyond the pale, since it implies a regimented and unimaginative ordinariness. (It's like calling a novelist a hack.) Appropriately, one of the finest purveyors of military medium in recent years was Matthew Fleming, who was an officer in the Royal Green Jackets for four years before joining Kent in 1989 and later winning eleven one-day international caps for England. But a career in Her Majesty's forces is no prerequisite.

See also BITS AND PIECES.

MILK

It might be what Ian Rush drinks, but that doesn't mean milk is confined to FOOTBALL. Surprisingly perhaps, milking has nothing to do with AGRICULTURAL batting or cow corner, and everything to do with playing the percentages, which has far more of an urban ring to it. If batsmen are scoring four or five singles an over without too much fuss, they are said to be milking the bowler. In other words, they are squeezing a steady trickle of runs out of him in the hope that the fielding captain will not throw the ball to someone more threatening. Bowlers who are milked are almost always spinners, and often in the middle overs of a one-day international. To accuse a fast bowler of lactating would, understandably, call into question his masculinity.

See also FIELDING POSITIONS; TWENTY20.

MYSTERY

A catch-all term that conveys English yearning for a spin bowler whose most dangerous weapon is not the ARM-BALL. The greatest advocate of mystery was Nasser Hussain, who longed for a bit of variety while he was captain of England. Instead, he got Chris Schofield, the Lancashire leg-spinner who was given a central contract at the age of twenty-one, took no wickets in his only two Tests, against Zimbabwe, and was released by his county in 2004. Bona fide mystery bowlers include Sonny Ramadhin, and the Australians Jack Iverson and John Gleeson.

See also CHUCKING; DOOSRA; GOOGLY; LEG-BREAK.

NELSON

Cricket's love of SUPERSTITION finds its most absurd expression in the score of 111 and its multiples (no, Nelson has nothing to do with Mandela or wrestling). These are known as Nelson, because the Admiral had one eye, one arm and one leg (except he had two legs, but no one has ever let that bother them too much). Pre-decimal bankers used the term to denote the sum of one pound, one shilling and one penny, but only cricket – ever the stickler – has clung to its quirk.

The former Test umpire David Shepherd believed that Nelson's evil powers could be combated by keeping his feet off the ground whenever the scoreboard revealed the dreaded figure, which must have made for a restless LUNCH when he officiated at Chennai in October 2004: on the first day of that game, Australia reached the interval at 111 without loss. But he need not have bothered. An analysis of Test batsmen who had – by the start of December 2005 – been dismissed between 100 and 118 shows that 111 is not unlucky at all: in fact, only 104 is luckier, with forty players losing their wicket for that score. A total of forty-five players had been out for 111, compared with sixty-one for 112, which suggests batsmen might subconsciously relax after moving past the supposed bogey score. Then again, since Nelson had two legs, perhaps 112 is the real bogey score after all.

Yet how are we to explain the bolt of lightning that

struck Trinidad & Tobago's Merv Dillon and the Windward Islands' Fernix Thomas at Kingston in October 2003? Both players had to receive treatment in hospital after complaining of headaches, tinnitus and burning sensations on the back of the neck. Needless to say, the lightning struck while the scoreboard was reading 111 for 7. On another occasion, a radio announcer could barely bring himself to utter the very figures. 'Yorkshire 232 all out,' he said. 'Len Hutton ill . . . No, I'm sorry: Len Hutton 111.'

The Australians are mystified by the fear of Nelson, despite having been skittled six times for that score, including the still-traumatic Headingley '81. For them, cricket's numerical albatross is 87 – possibly because it is thirteen short of 100, possibly because Keith Miller remembers as a young boy watching Don BRADMAN being dismissed for that score (in fact, he was out for 89, but the story is said to have spread). For some, Nelson was more of a dream than a nightmare: England batsmen of the 1980s had a particularly unfortunate relationship with the number 0. For others, it will always exercise something of a grip. Four players – the Australians Arthur Morris, Graeme Wood and Mark Waugh, and Taufeeq Umar of Pakistan – have been out twice for 111 in Tests. Gundappa Viswanath and Rahul Dravid of India, and New Zealand's Nathan Astle have fallen for 222. And England's Graham Gooch uniquely made 333, which tripped off the tongue so nicely that he immediately launched a range of bats bearing his score. Unlucky? Hardly.

See also ALL-ROUNDER; DUCK; FOLLOW-ON.

NERVOUS NINETIES

A self-explanatory phrase which disproves the view commonly expressed by batsmen that the gap between 99 and 100 is but a single run. On the contrary, it is a vast psychological chasm. 'Nervous' is probably the nicest way of putting it. The phenomenon is so common that Kersi Meher-Homji decided to write a book about it, and presciently asked Michael Slater to do the foreword. At the time, Slater had fallen in the nineties in Tests on three occasions for Australia, but by the end of his international career in 2001 that figure had risen to nine, breaking the West Indian Alvin Kallicharran's record by two (Kallicharran also finished not out in the nineties once). And if you think that getting out in the nineties has nothing to do with mental strength – or lack of it – consider this: in fifty-two Tests it was a fate that never befell Don BRADMAN.

See also YIPS.

NETS

The area where players practise all kinds of weird and wonderful manoeuvres, very few of which ever seem to appear in matches. When David Gower was England captain in the 1980s, the nets were generally known by their more technically correct name, which is 'naughty-boy nets'. The idea, roughly speaking, was that England's batsmen would not repeat the error of being skittled for 150 by some of the world's most ferocious bowlers on the Caribbean's most notorious terror-tracks if they went back to the nets and practised patting back HALF-VOLLEYS against club-standard medium-pacers. The idea did not quite stand up to scrutiny.

NICK

A nick is a very thin edge to the wicketkeeper. Batsmen can also nick – or pinch or steal – quick singles, a process known as rotating the strike and one which leaves the ex-pros who dominate the commentary boxes purring with approval.

See also SNICKOMETER.

NIGHTWATCHMAN

A lower-order batsman who goes in above his station just before the close of play to protect his more senior colleagues. Attitudes vary on the subject. Steve Waugh regarded the very notion as a slur on Australia's collective manhood, and banned the use of nightwatchmen while he was captain. But in *The Art of Captaincy* Mike Brear-ley notes that 'Middlesex once had a LUNCH-watchman,' before adding wisely, 'though that was before my time as captain.'

For those teams who do not regard the tactic as a flagrant act of cowardice, the choice of nightwatchman can be a tricky one. The batsman must be good enough to prevent further loss that evening, but not so good that his demise would feel like a major blow. More often than not, the nightwatchman will survive until stumps and then hang around for half an hour or so the next day. Occasionally, though, he can become a major irritant. Nasim-ul-Ghani, the Pakistani who batted in every position from opener to

No. 11 during his 29-match career, became not only the first nightwatchman to score a Test hundred when he made 101 against England at Lord's in 1962, but also the first Pakistani century-maker in England. He could not prevent defeat, however, which makes Tony Mann's 105 for Australia against India at Perth in December 1977 a more valuable nightwatchman's knock. Set 339 to win, Australia got there with two wickets to spare.

English nightwatchmen have had several near-misses. Harold Larwood spent most of the 1932–33 BODYLINE series scaring the life out of Australia's batsmen, but in the fifth Test at Sydney he made 98 batting at No. 4. Eddie Hemmings hit 95, also at Sydney, in January 1983, and Alex Tudor hit an unbeaten 99 in the win over New Zealand at Edgbaston in July 1999. Neither Larwood nor Hemmings made a Test century, and Tudor is unlikely ever to do so.

But the most astonishing example of a TAILender going beyond the call of duty came at Chittagong in April 2006, when Jason Gillespie, who had spent most of his Test career oscillating between No. 9 and 10 in the order, compiled an undefeated 201 in Australia's first innings of 581 for 4 declared. Gillespie's previous Test best had been 54 not out but now, batting at No. 3, he hung around for 574 minutes and 425 balls and boosted his AVERAGE from 15.64 to 18.73. 'This is ridiculous,' he laughed later. 'Absolutely fairytale.' A promise to team-mate Matthew Hayden to perform a nude lap of the Chittagong Divisional Stadium was mercifully scratched on the grounds of taste.

See also NERVOUS NINETIES; RABBIT; STREAKERS.

NOD

What you are deemed to have received from the selectors if you make the squad or final XI.

NUDGE

What you give to the selectors if you are making a strong case for a place in the squad or final XI. Alternatively, nudgers might be said to be knocking at the door – presumably to the dressing-room. Nudge is also what successful nudgers might do once they are out on the pitch and are looking for a risk-free single.

NURDLE

Not a word you'll find in the more concise dictionaries, but a highly evocative noun nonetheless. A nurdle is a shot played deftly and deliberately into gaps between fielders. It usually brings one or two runs, rather than three or four (and never six), and for some reason is often used to describe the batting of a left-hander: read any report of a long innings by Graham Thorpe and you have an even chance of stumbling across a nurdle or three, probably very near to NUDGE. Just don't get into a discussion about its meaning with a tiddlywinks aficionado. In that game, to nurdle means to shoot a wink so close to the pot that it can't be potted.

OFF-BREAK

The off-spinner's STOCK BALL. It TURNS, in theory at least, from off to leg and is delivered with a spin of the second and third fingers of the right hand as the WRIST rotates anti-clockwise as the batsman sees it. The Shane Warne-inspired leg-spin revolution has inspired many a dinner party to wonder whether conventional finger-spin is dead now that pitches are no longer left uncovered and at the mercy of the analysis-flattering elements. But such suggestions simply provide finger-spinners with the chance to demonstrate an alternative use for their second and third digits.

See also DOOSRA; GOOGLY; STICKY WICKET.

OLD FATHER TIME

He's as old as the stars, wears a long beard, carries a scythe and is about to spoil everyone's fun by pulling up the stumps. Yes, in days gone by Old Father Time would have made the perfect LORD's steward, but he missed his vocation and instead sits on top of the weathervane on the MOUND STAND, master of all he surveys. Ever since he was presented to the MCC by Sir Herbert Baker, who designed the old grandstand which was opened in 1926, Old Father Time has been a reassuring constant, although in 1940 he was briefly knocked from his perch by a cable belonging to one of the barrage balloons set up by the British Air Raid Precautions service to discourage dive-bombing by the Luftwaffe.

Returning to Lord's in 1948 to report on Don BRAD-MAN'S INVINCIBLES, the former Australia batsman Jack Fingleton captured something of his eternity: 'Old Father Time swings lazily and understandingly on his weather perch above the scoring-board as if another cricket season, as it is, is just another cricket season to him, and he will, without question, give it his benediction, blessing the centuries and the rich strokes and the clean-bowleds and understanding, with his hoary experience, the discomfiture of the man dismissed at Lord's for nothing.'

Some say he is only marginally older than the average MCC member, but that's being a little unfair on Old Father Time, who is lent a positively youthful air by the 23.5-carat gold leaf which decorates his scythe, as well as the ball which lies by the soon-to-be-drawn stumps, the vane itself and the four cardinal points. And yet he outlives all cricketers, even if there must occasionally have been some doubt in 1990 while New Zealand's Trevor Franklin was compiling a Test hundred in 7 hours and 11 minutes.

See also LONG ROOM; STONEWALL.

ONE-DAY INTERNATIONAL

If you were taking home a form of cricket to meet your parents for the first time, you'd probably choose a Test match: serious, subtle, respected, and with long-term prospects. The one-day international is probably best left in the bar: brash, loud, potentially exciting but essentially dull, he is unlikely to linger in the memory. Yet in the subcontinent and South Africa, it is the one-day game which packs out the grounds as fans come in search of big hits and instant gratification.

The first one-day international took place by accident. Australia and England had been scheduled to play the third Test of the 1970–71 ASHES at Melbourne, but rain wiped out the first three days so the authorities decided to entertain the crowd by staging a one-day game consisting of forty eight-ball overs a side instead. England made a naive 190, before Australia replied with 191 for 5 with five overs to spare. The second one-day international did not take place for another twenty months (Dennis Amiss hit the format's first century to help England to a six-wicket win over Australia at Old Trafford), and the ripple soon spread. The first World Cup was staged in England in 1975, but it needed the intervention of Kerry PACKER's World Series Cricket two years later to introduce the loud-mouthed, pyjama-wearing larrikin we know and love today.

One-day internationals are now so common – the game between Ireland, making their first appearance at senior level, and England in Belfast on 13 June 2006 was the 2,383rd – that they are often abbreviated to ODI, although some pedants prefer LOI (limited-overs internationals) on the grounds that occasionally a game will be forced into a second day by the weather. They are also pretty unmemorable, with the notable exception of Australia's TIE with South Africa in the semi-final of the 1999 World Cup at Edgbaston. Lance Klusener had brought the scores level in the last over of the match by clubbing Damien Martyn's first two balls through the covers for four, but when he called No. 11 Allan Donald through for what was supposed to be the winning single two balls later, Donald failed to hear the call, then dropped his bat. Australia went through by dint of a better record in the previous stage of the competition, and Donald wondered whether he'd ever be allowed back into South Africa again.

See also DUCKWORTH/LEWIS METHOD, THE; HELMETS; MILK; TWENTY20.

ORIGINS

When did cricket begin? Ask the old question about the length of a piece of string and you are likely to get a more definitive answer. 'The origins of cricket lie somewhere in the Dark Ages – probably after the Roman Empire, almost certainly before the Normans invaded England, and almost certainly somewhere in Northern Europe.' So says *WISDEN*, and if that's as precise as they can be, then GOD help the rest of us. *Wisden* explains that cricket's development in medieval times has been attributed to 'high-born country landowners, *émigré* Flemish cloth-workers, shepherds on the close-cropped downland of south-east England and the close-knit communities of iron- and glass-workers deep in the Kentish Weald'. In fact, the only groups we can safely say did not invent the game are the Inuits, the Mongol hordes, and the Scots.

There is, though, evidence that the game was played in Guildford, Surrey, around 1550. Was this a case of members of the original stockbroker belt seeking to amuse themselves while waiting for the 07.45 horse and cart into Waterloo? Alas, no: it seems to refer to a claim made by Mr John Derrick to his childhood games of 'kreckett'. In 1598, cricket gets a mention in John Florio's Italian–English dictionary. And in 1611 Randle Cotgrave's French–English version translates 'crosse' as 'cricket staff'. *Wisden* says the first reference to a cricket match played abroad was in 1676, when a bunch of Brits raised eyebrows in the Syrian town of Aleppo. Kent played Surrey in 1709 – the first recorded county match – and the game has never looked back, except when it is unhappy with the present and wants to wallow in the past, which happens more or less every week.

OVER

MAIDENS aren't what they used to be. It's easier to join the DOTS in these days of six-ball overs, but until 1979–80 in Australia and New Zealand bowlers would have to toil through eight deliveries before they could take a breather. A century earlier, an over consisted of only four balls, but that changed to five in 1889, and then to six in 1900. But as the batsmen began to dominate in the 1920s and '30s, so life became tougher for the bowlers: eight-ball overs were introduced in Australia (in 1922), New Zealand (1924), and South Africa (1937). The lily-livered Poms stuck with six.

No bowler can send down two consecutive overs, but Australia's captain Warwick Armstrong was never one to be overly troubled by the Laws. During the 1921 ASHES Test at Old Trafford, England DECLARED illegally – back then you were not allowed to do so on the first day after 100 minutes before the close – and play was held up for twenty minutes as the umpires and captains dissected the regulations. Armstrong had bowled the last over before the break, and proceeded to bowl the first after it, without anyone noticing. Since Armstrong's sheer size earned him the nickname 'The Big Ship', this was quite a feat.

But if it takes one Australian to bowl two overs, how many West Indians do you need? At Kandy in November

2001, the answer was four. Pedro Collins completed the fourth over of the match, before Merv Dillon began the fifth, only to leave the field after two balls because he was feeling unwell. He was replaced by Colin Stuart, who was removed from the attack by the umpires after two of his first three deliveries (both of them no-balls) turned out to be BEAMERS. So it was left to the off-spinner Chris Gayle to complete the over. West Indies eventually lost by 131 runs.

PACKER, KERRY (1937–2005)

Kerry Francis Bullmore Packer. Nearly thirty years after he changed the sport for ever, there were members of the cricket establishment who remained incapable of uttering his name without looking as if they had just been hit in the groin and forgotten to wear a BOX. A business tycoon with the frame of an ox and the hide of a rhino, Packer famously set out his agenda – to gain exclusive TV rights of Australian cricket for his own Channel Nine station – at a meeting with the Australian Cricket Board in June 1976. 'Come on now, we're all harlots,' he said in a silver-tongued attempt to persuade the ACB to look beyond their long-standing relationship with the Australian Broadcasting Corporation. 'Name your price.' Although Packer was offering well over double the pitch from the ABC, the answer from the Board was not the one he wanted to hear.

Packer's response was to flex his financial muscle and buy up scores of the world's best players – including the captains of England (Tony Greig), Australia (Greg Chappell) and West Indies (Clive Lloyd) – for a series of self-consciously gladiatorial battles which he grandly called World Series Cricket. Back at LORD'S, the suits were not happy, and following England's victory in the 1977 Ashes, the ICC announced a ban on any cricketer 'who has played, or made himself available to play, in a match previously disapproved by the Conference'. Packer and Greig contested the ruling and won a famous case in the high court, where the judge decided that the ICC's ban represented an unreasonable restraint of trade.

Packer celebrated by dressing his new employees in coloured clothing (the West Indian XI wore an eye-watering salmon pink), and introducing floodlights, white balls, black SIGHTSCREENS and gaudy jingles. Detractors referred to the whole thing as a circus, but if the players looked like clowns, at least they were being paid handsomely for the privilege. 'What he improved was cricket's ability to exploit its popularity commercially,' wrote Gideon Haigh, shortly after Packer's death on Boxing Day 2005.

WSC lasted only until 1979, but by then Packer's remark about harlots had proved correct: he had secured three years' worth of TV rights, plus a ten-year deal to market the game in Australia. WSC was no longer necessary, but its spirit lives on, and Packer would one day be named by Cricket Australia (the new name for the ACB) as the second-most influential figure in Australian cricket, behind only Don BRADMAN. Not bad for a man who, in the eyes of cricket's administrators, once ranked second only to the devil.

See also ONE-DAY INTERNATIONAL.

PARTY, COMING TO THE

International cricket is supposed to be a serious business, yet anyone who has scored runs, taken wickets or held catches is said by their captain or coach to have 'come to the party'. Where this party is, and whether you need to bring a bottle or in FANCY DRESS as Elvis, is unclear. What matters is that the player in question has done his bit for the team. Alternatively, he might be said to have 'put his hand up', 'stood up and been counted', or 'stepped up to the plate', a lazy plagiarism from baseball.

PENCIL CRICKET

In most cases it began in the back row of the history class. Before long it was an obsession. Soon everyone was doing it, even one or two of the cool kids. The beauty of pencil cricket was that whole Test matches could be won and lost in the time it took to learn about the causes of the First World War or the spread of the bubonic plague. All you needed were two six-sided pencils, a notebook and the ability to stare intently at the blackboard while logging the progress of the ASHES decider that was being enacted under your nose. The sole flaw in this testimony to restless youth was the scoring system. With only six options – 6, 4, 3, 2, 1 and Howzat! – on one pencil (the other pencil contained the outcome of the appeal), the runs flowed like the semolina in the school canteen. This was TWENTY20 before its time. It also explains why some British children's historical knowledge fails to extend beyond 1066.

In the cricket clubs of apartheid South Africa, the pencil was a symbol of oppression rather than liberation, even in the black cricket leagues, where fairer skin was more likely to get you a game. To determine whether a player was 'coloured' – to use the terminology of the regime – or black, a pencil would be placed in his HAIR: if it fell through, he would be regarded as coloured; if it stayed put, he was a black, and would probably be shunned.

PINCH-HITTING

In baseball a pinch-hitter is a substitute brought on in

emergencies specifically to launch the ball out of the park. Cricket has subverted the definition subtly, using it to describe a batsman sent in up the order to give a one-day innings a kickstart. Traditionalists call it SLOGGING; pragmatists couldn't care less.

The general wisdom is that cricket's first bout of successful pinch-hitting was carried out at the 1996 World Cup by the Sri Lankan openers Sanath Jayasuriya, who smashed his runs at the heady rate of 132 per 100 balls, and Romesh Kaluwitharana. But this interpretation usually overlooks the fact that sixteen other batsmen in the competition scored more runs than Jayasuriya, while Kaluwitharana AVERAGED only 12. It is also harsh on New Zealand's Mark Greatbatch, who at the previous World Cup in 1992 had biffed his way to 313 runs off only 356 balls. And you could even make a case for calling India's Kris Srikkanth the first career pinch-hitter: he spent most of the 1980s opening in one-day internationals *and* Tests with outrageous swash and buckle.

What Jayasuriya and Kaluwitharana did achieve, however, was to change the way teams approached a one-day innings. In the days before pinch-hitting, sides would look to accumulate slowly before going for broke in the final ten overs. After 1996, the feeling was that the first fifteen overs – when the fielding restrictions were in place and the gaps in the outfield inviting – represented a chance to make hay. It's all a far cry from 1970–71, when the first one-day international took place at Melbourne, and the England opener Geoff Boycott made 8 off 37 balls. These days, such caution might arouse the interest of the ICC's Anti-Corruption Unit. Back then Boycs was probably applauded for taking the shine off the new ball.

See also HAIR; MATCH-FIXING; USA.

PLUMB

Almost always used of LEG BEFORE WICKET decisions, when the appeal is so obviously a good one that even the batsman knows he is out. 'That's plumb!' is a common scream in the commentary box, seconds before the umpire furiously shakes his head and indicates that the batsman got an inside edge. A plumb pitch is perfect for batting, but the usage is going the same way as 'jeepers' and 'crikey', unless your name is Mark Nicholas.

PRESS CONFERENCE

A strange ritual in which JOURNALISTS ask players questions to which they already know the answers, and players respond as if they have been asked to divulge the secrets of the Da Vinci Code. The result is a tedious circle: the more the hacks probe, the more defensive the players become, so the more the hacks probe . . . In the end, you are left with quotes you could have written without being there: 'looking forward to the challenge' . . . '110 per cent' . . . 'under no illusions' . . . '150 per cent' . . . 'I wouldn't know about that' . . . '2,000 per cent'. Journalists still turn up in the vain hope that someone might say something interesting, while the sole aim of the players is to get through the grilling without putting their foot in it. The two goals tend to be mutually exclusive.

PRESSURE

Pressure can do funny things to a man. He might even start blathering about 'pressure cricket', as if it were a new form of the game, like TWENTY20. West Indies used to respond to claims that their fast bowlers were making life uncomfortable for opposition batsmen by saying, 'If you can't stand the heat, get out of the kitchen,' which was another way of saying their preferred method of food preparation was to use the pressure cooker. At times, Michael Vaughan seemed incapable of getting through an interview without stressing the need to put Australia/Bangladesh/the tea lady under pressure. But according to Keith Miller, the flamboyant Australia ALL-ROUNDER who fought in the war and was said to have rerouted one mission so he could fly over Bonn and see the birthplace of Beethoven, 'Pressure is a Messerschmitt up your arse.' Hard to argue with, really.

See also CHARACTER; CUTLERY.

PUDDING

Not merely a county stalwart's favourite part of the day (along with LUNCH and TEA), but a slow, low pitch whose texture might, if you were feeling particularly colourful, be compared to Victoria sponge. Puddings are always found in England, and usually in the Midlands.

PULL

Cricketers go on the pull a lot. But the very best succeed *on* the pitch as well as off it. The pull shot – a cross-batted hit to leg against the short ball – is a useful way to keep the bowler in his place. Not only does it tell him that the batsman has picked up the length of the delivery very early (implying that the bowler simply isn't fast enough to trouble him), but it oozes confidence. Most pull shots are played against short-pitched balls, but the most exhilarating make mincemeat of deliveries which are only just short of a good length. In 2002–03, Michael Vaughan introduced Australian crowds to his swivel-pull, where the back leg adopts an elegantly half-cocked position that only infuriates the bowler further. But as with all leg-side shots, the criticism is fierce if the pull costs you your wicket. It is this hint of reckless-ness that makes it such an attractive stroke.

PURPLE PATCH

Purple patches come in all shapes and sizes, but only one colour. If you find yourself in the middle of one you are probably a batsman who can't stop scoring runs, rather than an eccentric with a Ribena fetish. Not surprisingly, Don BRADMAN boasts one of the three purplest patches in the history of the game. In successive FIRST-CLASS innings in 1938–39, he scored 118, 143, 225, 107, 186 and 135 not out. Needing one more hundred to beat C. B. Fry's all-time record, set in 1901, Bradman was out for 5 against Victoria, confirming suspicions that he was little more than a flash in the pan. Thirty-two years later, the feats of Fry and Bradman were equalled by Mike Procter, playing for Rhodesia. In 2003, Northamptonshire's captain, Mike Hussey, came close, hitting 100, 331 not out, 115, 187 and 147 in consecutive championship knocks, only to fall for 50 in the second innings against Glamorgan. That hint of mental weakness must have been why the Australian selectors ignored him for so long.

See also ALBANIA; AVERAGES; GOLDEN AGE.

QUEEN, THE

The royal family tend to turn their noses up at sports that do not involve horses, but cricket has come as close as any activity to breaking the equine monopoly. The reigning monarch used to meet and greet the two teams at every LORD's Test, after which tradition dictated that a wicket would fall immediately, except when Don BRADMAN was batting (he only ever bent the knee to Harold Larwood).

In 1972, after Bob Massie had demolished England in 3½ days – the match finished before TEA on the fourth day, which is when the royal hand was usually shaken – the Australians were invited to Buckingham Palace instead. At one with the world after a few celebratory drinks, Dennis Lillee greeted Queen Elizabeth with 'G'day!' On another occasion, he asked her for her autograph during the Centenary Test at Melbourne in March 1977. She declined at the time, explaining that it might set a tiring precedent, but later sent him a photo signed 'Elizabeth R, 1977'. 'You can imagine how chuffed I was,' enthused Lillee.

In terms of cricket knowledge, Elizabeth II takes a back throne to her husband, Prince Philip, who has twice served as president of the MCC and had also been greeted with a Lillee 'G'day!' back in 1972. Philip was invited to stand as president of The Lord's Taverners, a charitable organization which raises money for the grass-roots game, but reportedly said it sounded too much like hard work. When it was put to him that he might like to be official twelfth man instead, 'to clean the kit, carry the drinks and generally stay in the pavilion and get sloshed', he was more excited. 'Excellent idea!' came the reply.

Philip's tendency to tread the line between good taste and bad has not spared cricket either. Following the shooting of sixteen schoolchildren and their teacher at Dunblane Primary School in 1996 and subsequent calls for gun ownership to be banned completely, he delicately remarked: 'If a cricketer, for instance, suddenly decided to go into a school and batter a lot of people to death with a cricket bat, which he could do very easily, I mean, are you going to ban cricket bats?'

Philip could actually play a bit, but probably the most talented cricketer in royal circles was George VI, who can lay claim to the most distinguished HAT-TRICK in the history of the game. Playing on the private grounds of Windsor Castle, the then Prince Albert bowled King Edward VII, the future King George V and the Prince of Wales, later to become Edward VIII, with successive deliveries, thus sparing the umpire the possibly treasonous task of giving them out lbw. The hat-trick ball can still be found in the mess room at the Royal Naval College in Dartmouth. George VI knew a little about the game too. When he and the Queen hosted the 1948 Australians at Balmoral, he asked the team scorer: 'Tell me, Mr Ferguson, do you use an adding machine when the Don comes to bat?'

These days, the royal presence makes itself felt whenever England play Australia, thanks to the BARMY ARMY. Their hilarious rendition of 'GOD Save Your Gracious Queen' is regularly directed at the Australian fans, thus doing wonders for England's reputation as a post-colonial haven for the open-minded. The Army are also responsible for the regular homage that has been paid to the King of Spain ever since a set of Ashley Giles souvenir mugs appeared in the Warwickshire club shop with a glorious typing error. The inscription was supposed to read 'The King of Spin'. 'Viva España', normally the ditty of choice of British housewives on the Costa del Sol, now echoed round the Test venues of England.

See also ALUMINIUM; BODYLINE; BRADMAN, SIR DONALD; INVINCIBLES; LEG BEFORE WICKET; SWING; WHEELIE BIN.

RABBIT

Rabbits – the disparaging name given to inept batsmen – are so called because they spend most of their time in the hutch, as the pavilion is known for the sake of this metaphor. It's all a little unfair really. After all, you wouldn't tell a scrum-half he was suddenly playing at prop, so why thrust a bat into the trembling hands of a rabbit and frogmarch him out to the middle to meet his inevitable doom? Because it's quite funny, that's why.

In any other sport, gross incompetence would be frowned upon. In cricket, it breeds folk heroes. Until Andrew Flintoff hit the big time, no other England bats-man would receive a louder cheer as he emerged from the pavilion than Devon Malcolm, who barely knew one end of the bat from the other. Malcolm's only regret must have been that he was not part of the legendary England TAIL of Alan Mullally, Phil Tufnell and Ed Giddins, who between them scored nine runs in six innings during the defeat to New Zealand at The Oval in August 1999.

Test cricket's most enduring rabbit, though, was the West Indian Courtney Walsh, whose tally of forty-three DUCKS was, by the end of 2005, well ahead of his near-est rivals. But there was one set of criteria in which even Walsh was out-rabbited: his compatriot Merv Dillon regis-tered ducks in twenty-six of his sixty-eight Test innings for a record percentage of 38 (Walsh's figure was a rela-tively respectable, but still utterly useless, 23).

In modern times, the battle for the title of Biggest Bunny has boiled down to two men. The Northampton-shire seamer Jim Griffiths, who retired in 1986, failed to score in fifty-one of his 138 first-class innings, and was even described by his own testimonial brochure as the 'Wally of the WILLOW'. His first-class batting AVERAGE of 3.33 hinted at depths most of us can only have nightmares about. But his mantle was taken up at Northants by Mark Robinson, who in 1990 did not break his duck in twenty of his twenty-five visits to the crease. At one stage Robin-son went thirteen innings – and four months – in the county championship without scoring a single run, and there were huge cheers when he got off the mark in the final of the NatWest Trophy against Lancashire. 'You'd have thought that was his first run since May,' joked Tony Lewis on the BBC commentary, unwittingly hitting the nail squarely on the head. Years later, Robinson would spoil all his hard work by making 27 for his new county, Sussex, leaving bitter Northants fans to wonder whether the summer of 1990 had been one long joke at their expense. He eventually retired with a first-class average of 4.01 and more runs (590) than wickets (584) – statis-tics which put Griffiths (290 runs, 444 wickets) firmly in his place.

See also FERRET; NELSON; SHOULDER ARMS.

RADAR

Radars, it seems, only ever malfunction. If a fast bowler with a reputation for occasional profligacy sprays the ball all over the place, it is because his 'radar is wonky' or 'awry', as if his opening spell of 5-0-38-0 were not his fault at all. But when the radar is in perfect working order, it barely gets a mention, which is probably sensible. If any reporter had congratulated Devon Malcolm on his figures of 9 for 57 against South Africa at The Oval in 1994 by saying, 'Well done, Dev, the radar worked a treat today, my old son,' the PRESS CONFERENCE might well have lasted about as long as one of Malcolm's own innings.

See also GRACE, W. G.; STOCK BALL.

RAIN

Most commonly seen before the words 'stops play' and the blight of venues such as Georgetown, Colombo, Dunedin and – ignore the protestations of the locals – Manchester. But it's not all bad news, or at least it wasn't when the BBC used to own the rights to home Tests and would take advantage of rain breaks to show reruns of Headingley '81, which seemed to be on a continuous spool in a little room at Broadcasting House. While most of us enjoyed revelling in the heroics of Ian Botham and Bob Willis, a man called Mike Hulme decided it was high time someone actually analysed the weather in Britain and told the cricket establishment that their scheduling was all wrong. According to research carried out by Hulme in 1989, the ideal six-Test home summer – one, that is, with the fewest interruptions for rain – would look like this: Headingley (starting on 1 June), Edgbaston (15 June), LORD's (13 July), Trent Bridge (27 July), Old Trafford (24 August), The Oval (7 September). So the next time you're sitting in Manchester in June and the heavens open and someone says, 'You can't blame anyone for the weather,' take them to task.

See also ALL-ROUNDER; DUCKWORTH/LEWIS METHOD, THE; FOLLOW-ON; GLOOM; LIGHT METERS; UMBRELLA.

REARGUARD

One of the idiosyncratic joys of a five-day sport that requires no resolution is the rearguard action, in which batsmen defend for as long as possible in the usually vain hope of salvaging a draw. But they do so in the knowledge that success will guarantee them a place in sporting-magazine list pieces ('Top 10 Back-Heels', 'Best-Ever Returns of Serve' – you know the sort of thing) for ever more.

No. 1 in the list of Greatest Rearguards is Hanif Mohammad, who rolled up his sleeves with unparalleled determination at Bridgetown in January 1958. As Pakistan FOLLOWED ON, a massive 473 behind West Indies on first innings, Hanif set about compiling 337 in a back-breaking 970 minutes, sharing stands of 152 for the first wicket with Imtiaz Ahmed, 112 for the second with Alimuddin, 154 for the third with Saeed Ahmed, and 121 for the fourth with Wazir Mohammad. When Pakistan finally DECLARED on 657 for 8, they had batted for 319 overs, the game was safe, and West Indian fielders were wandering around like zombies.

It was not the first time they had been denied by backs placed stubbornly against the wall. At Edgbaston in June 1957, Peter May and Colin Cowdrey put on 411 for the fourth wicket to make amends for England's first-innings deficit of 288. May hit an undefeated 285 in ten hours, and Cowdrey 154 in ten minutes short of 8½, before England took seven quick West Indian wickets to flirt with a stunning win. Their partnership is often credited with the introduction of pad-play, a cynical but perfectly legal ploy used by May and Cowdrey to nullify the threat of Sonny Ramadhin, who had taken 7 for 49 in the first innings with his mixed bag of spinners. In the second, Ramadhin claimed only 2 wickets and needed 98 overs to get them – his tally of 774 deliveries in the match was the most by any bowler in a Test. He never claimed five wickets in an innings for West Indies again.

In fact, the English seem to figure quite highly in the rearguard annals, which might say something about their ability to poop a party. In June 1953, Trevor Bailey and Willie Watson kept a nation on tenterhooks with a stand of 163 in over four hours on the last day of the second Test to deny Australia. Without that draw, England might not have regained the ASHES they had last won twenty years earlier under Douglas Jardine. And at Johannesburg in December 1995, Mike Atherton batted for 643 minutes to make 185 not out and save England's bacon against South Africa. Only Len Hutton (364 in 797 minutes *v* Australia at The Oval in 1938), Ken Barrington (256 in 683 *v* Australia at Old Trafford in 1964) and Clive Radley (158 in 648 *v* New Zealand at Auckland in 1977–78) had played longer innings for England. And none of them had to do it, as Atherton did, with Jack Russell (29 not out in 274 minutes) constantly yapping in his ear.

A year later, cricketing karma struck as only cricketing karma can. Atherton's team had two sessions in which to take the final New Zealand wicket and wrap up a comfortable win at Auckland, but they were denied by an unbroken last-ditch stand of 106 between Nathan Astle and the fantastically incompetent Danny Morrison, who failed to score in twenty-four of his seventy-one Test innings and

issued a commemorative tie replete with DUCKS to celebrate the fact. Now, egged on by Astle, Morrison lunged
forward for 166 balls and 133 minutes to score 14 not out
and secure a draw. His reward? He was dropped for the
next Test and never played for his country again.

See also BODYLINE; CALYPSO CRICKET; CHUCKING;
INITIALS; MASTER, THE; MICHELLE; STONEWALL.

RED INK

The colour used by scorers to denote a not-out innings.
Fighting to preserve your wicket is, of course, one of the
fundamentals of the game, but cricketers who are overly
fond of red ink – and, by extension, their own batting
AVERAGE – are easy prey for SLEDGERS. When the Australia
wicketkeeper Ian Healy wanted to hurry things along during
the 1993 Ashes Test at Edgbaston, he responded to a defensive shot from Graham Thorpe by announcing: 'Hey! You
know what? This guy's playing for red ink . . .' (At least that
was the pre-watershed version that appeared in Thorpe's
autobiography.) Moments later, red ink was replaced by red
mist as Thorpe was stumped trying to launch Shane Warne
into Birmingham city centre – the only time in his 100-Test
career, he says, that SLEDGING directly cost him his wicket.

It stands to reason that the three players with the most
Test not-outs all bat or batted at No. 11, where the theor-
etical chances of red ink are an enticing 50–50. Courtney
Walsh (batting average: 7.54) was unbeaten in a record 61
of his 185 innings, while Bob Willis (11.50) is next with 55
out of 128, an even higher ratio. Third and on the rise all
the time is Glenn McGrath, who achieved his 49th splash
of red ink by making 1 not out against South Africa at

Sydney in January 2006, a run that lifted his average from 7.50 to 7.51, and was thus not to be sniffed at.

But the presence of four top-order batsmen in Test cricket's top 20 all-time not-outers provides a revealing insight into the mindset of the habitual red-inker. Steve Waugh (46 not-outs in 260 knocks) is fourth, while his fellow Aussie battler Allan Border (44 in 265) is fifth. Lower down the list come South Africa's Jacques Kallis (28 in 161 following McGrath's game at Sydney) and, yes, Thorpe (28 in 179). All four players are or were known for their tenacity, which most interpreted as grit, a few as selfishness.

In the one-day arena, red ink is a less ambiguous badge of honour, providing you have made the most of your time at the CREASE. So it is no surprise that the player who has been painted red most times in one-day international history is Australia's Michael Bevan. His tally of 67 not-outs from 196 innings is only slightly less spectacular than his ODI average of 53.58 – a BRADMANesque figure in the shorter form of the game.

See also BOUNCER; DUCK; ONE-DAY INTERNATIONAL; RABBIT.

ROUGH

A bit of rough is not the sort of thing that is likely to excite most cricketers, unless it is a few feet outside the right-hander's leg-stump, the opposition need 200 to win on the last day, and your spin bowler is called Shane Warne. Rough is what is created by a seamer's boots when he follows through down the pitch after delivering the ball. Spinners bowling from the other end will then look to exploit the worn patches in the hope that batting becomes something of a lottery. This is praised as a masterful tactic when applied by most teams, but pilloried as typical English defensiveness when purveyed by Phil Tufnell or Ashley Giles.

The rough plays such an important psychological part in the progress of a five-day game that sides will go to almost any lengths to ensure it does not feel neglected. Fielders in the deep will routinely aim the ball in front of the stumps so that the wicketkeeper has to run onto the pitch to gather the return (and possibly nurture the rough with his studs), while batsmen in the third innings of a game will find all sorts of excuses to march up and down between deliveries, turning neatly on their heels as if in a North Korean military parade. But the most blatant piece of roughery came from Shahid Afridi during Pakistan's draw with England at Faisalabad in November 2005. Taking advantage of the chaos caused by an exploding soft-drinks machine on the BOUND-ARY, Afridi casually walked on to the pitch and performed a pirouette that would have put Rudolf Nureyev to shame. The cameras, though, were still watching and Afridi was banned for one Test and two one-day internationals for his 'moment of madness'. Old pros everywhere could not believe his stupidity: the golden rule about roughing up the pitch is never, under any circumstances, get caught.

See also WONDERBALL.

RUGBY

Cricket's competition as Britain's second sport behind FOOTBALL. We try not to talk about it, except when England are beating Australia.

See also ASHES, THE.

SEAM

The stitching round the middle of the ball is not just there for decorative reasons. Depending on how pronounced it is, the seam should provide help to the seamers, the bowlers whose principal weapon is the movement they derive from landing the ball on the strands of string that hold it together. English bowlers have traditionally been over-reliant on help from the seam, and there was outcry when the Test and County Cricket Board (which later became the England and WALES Cricket Board) reduced the number of strands from fifteen in 1989 to nine in 1990. The predictable upshot was a summer of fun for the batsmen: a typical county scoreboard that year came at The Oval, where Lancashire made 863 in reply to Surrey's 707 for 9 declared. The quarter-seam runs perpendicular to the main seam, and both are ripe for illegal manipulation by bowlers desperate to redress what they regard as the game's innate imbalance between bat and ball. Batsmen call this cheating; bowlers believe it is a necessary evil.

See also BALL-TAMPERING; DECLARATIONS.

SHARJAH

Take a magnifying glass to an atlas, and zoom in on the part of the world where the Persian Gulf turns into the

Strait of Hormuz. Perched on the coast is the state of Sharjah, which in 1971 became part of the United Arab Emirates and has seen more international cricket than anywhere else outside the boundaries of the Test-playing nations. Sharjah's stadium has shades of Las Vegas: built in the desert, it is essentially an ode to commercialism masquerading as fun for all the family (minus the women and children). Men dressed as Elvis Presley, though, are thinner on the ground.

Matches first took place at Sharjah in 1981 thanks to the fund-raising efforts of Abdulrahman Bukhatir, an Arab businessman who fell in love with the game while he was a student in Pakistan. Spurred on by generous match fees and the presence of thousands of subcontinental ex-pats, India were regular visitors, but it was the Pakistanis who really forged a bond with Sharjah, coming back year after year like Brits to Benidorm. Their fondness for this patch of desert was consummated in April 1986 when Javed Miandad hit Chetan Sharma's last ball of the match for six to send India into mourning. And when opponents grew wary of travelling to Pakistan in the first few years of the new millennium because of concerns over safety, the matches were moved to Sharjah instead. Pakistan were so grateful that in one game they even allowed Australia to bowl them out for 59 and 53.

For Pakistan it became a home away from home. For the non-Asian nations, it was an occasional chore. Many also suspected Sharjah was the spiritual home of MATCH-FIXING, which might explain why the last tournament staged there was the fragrant-sounding Cherry Blossom Cup in April 2003. But its proximity to Iraq did not help either.

Still, Sharjah helped put the United Arab Emirates on

the cricketing map, although anyone who watched the UAE take part in the 1996 World Cup will wonder whether this was such a good thing. Their captain, Sultan Mohammed Zarawani, famously emerged to face South Africa's Allan Donald wearing only a floppy hat (no, that doesn't mean he was naked). He was hit on the head first ball. Zarawani could at least boast that he was the only native in a side full of imports, but his final one-day international stats (a batting AVERAGE of 4.33, a bowling average of 51) suggested that he probably shouldn't have given up the day job, assuming he had one.

See also FANCY-DRESS; HELMETS.

SHIRTFRONT

Like a FEATHERBED, but more austere. While the featherbed conveys warmth and cosiness, the shirtfront – a pitch so flat it might have been ironed – almost implies a moral obligation to score runs by conjuring up images of Victorian gents in top hats and starched collars.

SHOCKER

The shocker is cricket's great leveller. No one is immune to its powers, from the beach player who trips over a dozing granny while taking a running catch into the sun, to the Test captain who wins the TOSS on a Birmingham belter and promptly says, 'We'll have a bowl, thanks, Mark.' Umpires tend to be attributed more shockers than any other breed, usually by fans of the team whose star batsman has just been given out caught off the peak of his HELMET. Thereafter, aggrieved observers – see worshippers of Sachin Tendulkar – will need no excuse whatsoever to discern a conspiracy theory and demand the instant removal of the umpire from the ICC's elite panel. Bowlers are more likely to endure shockers than batsmen, who tend not to last long if they are out of form. By contrast, the bowlers cannot retreat to the pavilion if they send down a bad ball, unless they feign injury. But then that would be even more of a shocker than having a shocker itself.

See also MASTER, THE.

SHOULDER ARMS

It sounds like a paradox, but it's actually quite tedious. To shoulder arms is to leave the ball alone outside off-stump by raising your arms high above your head. Jack Russell used to try to turn what was essentially a decisive act of defence into an irritating gesture by holding the pose and staring back at the bowler through his inscrutable shades. Courtney Walsh shouldered arms with a flourish, possibly because he could do very little else, while Dermot Reeve once took the bat out of the equation entirely by throwing it away repeatedly as he padded up to Hampshire's left-arm spinner Raj Maru. The Laws were later amended to prevent a repeat of this rather cynical piece of ingenuity, with the MCC arguing that the flying bat might get in the way of an attempt to catch the ball, thus rendering the batsman open to being dismissed for obstructing the field.

See also ANALYST, THE; DISMISSALS; DRUGS; DUCK; RABBIT.

SIGHTSCREEN

A bit of a sledgehammer to crack a nut. The sightscreen is huge, but its only purpose is to allow batsmen to see the tiny red ball against its pristine whiteness (or, in day/night cricket, the white ball against its grim blackness). If a batsman is unlucky, the bowler will be so tall that the ball is delivered from above the level of the sightscreen (see Curtly Ambrose and Joel Garner). If he is very unlucky, the spectator sitting just behind the sightscreen, but in the batsman's line of vision, will be wearing an unfeasibly large red hat. This is one of the rare occasions on which a cricketer will swear at a lady.

See also ECONOMY; PACKER, KERRY; SLEDGING.

SITTER

Few phenomena in sport are as cruel as the fluffed sitter – a catch so simple that, in the words of Geoff Boycott, 'My mum could have caught that in her pinny.' Of course, genuine sitters (or dollies) are few and far between at Test level, where PRESSURE can turn even the safest pair of hands into a pair of oil-greased saucepans. But catches are always easier to take from the safety of the corporate or commentary boxes, and drops have a way of attracting the sort of attention with which FOOTBALL goalkeepers are all too familiar.

Bowl a bad over and you can always come back for a second spell. Play a bad shot and you might get a second innings. But drop, shell, grass, fluff or spill a sitter and you can be stigmatized for life. The England bowler Fred

Tate won only one Test cap, but the game in question – against Australia at Old Trafford in July 1902 – became known as Tate's Match, largely because he dropped Joe Darling on the square-leg fence at a crucial stage of Australia's second innings. When Tate was last man out, bowled with four runs needed for victory, his fate was sealed. But it was the sitter that did the damage, and he was never picked again.

As Tate discovered, the cruellest mistakes are the ones which assume an even greater importance in retrospect. At Headingley in July 1997 Graham Thorpe dropped Matthew Elliott at first slip with the ASHES delicately poised. Elliott had 29 at the time, but his eventual 199 gave Australia a series lead they never relinquished. An even more clear-cut example occurred at The Oval in September 2005 when Shane Warne spilled an equally straightforward slip chance to reprieve Kevin Pietersen on 15. By the time Australia removed Pietersen for 158, the Ashes were back in English hands for the first time in eighteen years.

Reactions to dropped catches reveal a lot too. After South Africa's Andre Nel had put down Ricky Ponting at midwicket during the 2005 Boxing Day Test at Melbourne, he admitted with characteristic melodrama that he wanted to 'end myself'. Ponting had 17 at the time but went on to make 117 and set up an Australian win. *Schadenfreude* is rarely far away either. As the magnitude of Warne's drop off Pietersen gradually became clear, the Oval crowd taunted him at the BOUNDARY with cries of 'Warney's dropped the Ashes', while the stadium's giant screen did its part by zeroing in on his distraught features. And all because he had failed to react in a split-second, under intense pressure, in front of over 20,000 baying fans, to a little red missile hurtling towards his head at the speed of a BMW in the outside lane. Still, as the crowd pointed out, Warney *had* just dropped the Ashes . . .

SLEDGING

If you have ever played in a so-called friendly and a twelve-year-old member of the opposition squeaks: 'Right, boys, we're into the TAIL' as you shamble out to open the batting, then you will instinctively understand the power of sledging. In the 1960s, to sledge was to swear in mixed company: anyone uncouth enough to curse in front of a lady was deemed to be 'as subtle as a sledgehammer'. In his autobiography Ian Chappell, the Australia captain who rarely bothered much with subtlety himself, explained: 'A later generation of players, unaware of its origin, began to describe on-field antics as sledging and, with the help of the media, the meaning of the word has broadened.'

In other words, a sledge is now the fielding team's way of getting inside the batsman's mind. Since most professionals reckon top-class cricket is mainly a mental game anyway, it is a tactic which appears to make perfect sense, just like diving for a penalty, or using a hand in the ruck. If you are on the receiving end, it is cheating; but if you are dishing it out, it is merely gamesmanship.

For Australians, of course, sledging has traditionally been viewed as part of the second category. And it has not simply been confined to the field of play. 'Hey, leave our flies alone, Jardine,' shouted one wag in the crowd at the hated begetter of BODYLINE. 'They're the only flamin' friends you've got here.' And before Phil Tufnell gave it all up for the razzmatazz and home-loans ads of the celebrity circuit, he was asked by an Australian fan whether he could lend him his brain. The reason? 'I'm building an idiot.'

Another Australia captain, Mark Taylor, claimed that 90 per cent of on-field banter is actually designed to encourage the bowler and fielders, with 9 per cent intended for the batsman's hearing and no more than 1 per cent aimed directly at him. But under the leadership of his successor, Steve Waugh, Australia were more open about their intentions. Inspired by the tough-cookie example of his former captain Allan Border, Waugh cunningly rebranded sledging as 'mental disintegration' – a bit like scribbling out 'custard' and inking in 'vanilla sauce' – and encouraged his side to abuse the opposition with more relish than ever. Graeme Smith, later to become captain of South Africa, revealed how, on his Test debut against Australia at Cape Town, he was heckled all day by Matthew Hayden and Shane Warne, whose general advice apparently revolved around a four-letter word beginning with 'c'. Smith was criticized for telling tales out of school, but evidently decided that if you can't beat 'em, you're better off joining 'em: four years later, Michael Vaughan complained that Smith spent much of the South Africa–England series calling him 'queer'. Perhaps the Australians had called Smith 'camp'.

Occasionally, sledging transcends the sexual and the scatological. When the umpire Dickie Bird asked the Australian fast bowler Merv Hughes why he felt the need to scream at England's Graeme Hick, Hughes replied: 'Because he offended me in a former life.' But the most famous alleged sledge of recent times came from Steve Waugh during a crucial World Cup game against South Africa at Headingley in 1999. Waugh chipped a simple catch to midwicket, where Herschelle Gibbs spilled the ball in the act of celebrating the DISMISSAL. 'Hersch, you've just dropped the World Cup,' was Waugh's reported comment. But interviewed six years later by Australia's *Inside Cricket* magazine, Waugh came clean. 'I wasn't quite that clever. I just said: "Look, do you realize you've just cost your team the game."' Still, the one-liner – whatever it was – did the trick. 'I'm still suffering from flashbacks,' admitted Gibbs a few years later.

See also CHARACTER; RED INK.

SLOG

One of those words which likes to have its cake and eat it by rejoicing in two diametrically opposed definitions. A slog can be little more than a YAHOO, a mad mow which hopes to hit the ball into the next postal district. If you want to get under the skin of an aspiring batsman who likes to give the ball a whack, call him a slogger. The implication is that he is trying to compensate for a woeful lack of technique by swinging at everything that moves. Shahid Afridi, who once smashed a one-day international hundred off 37 balls for Pakistan against Sri Lanka, is often disparaged as a slogger, in which case he is an extremely high-class example. A slog can also be anything but. If the batsmen are struggling to get the ball off the SQUARE, then the commentator will inform viewers in between yawns that 'It's a real slog out there.' There ought to be few problems in distinguishing between the two meanings.

See also AGRICULTURE.

SLOWCOACH

Only in cricket could a player advertise his slowness and get away with it. Mark Richardson, the former New Zealand opener who turned himself from a left-arm spinner with the YIPS into one of the most bloody-minded batsmen in the world, was not the quickest in the outfield, which is a polite way of saying he could barely put one foot in front of the other. So in a typically good-natured bid to make a silk purse out of the ear of a very sluggish sow, Richardson decided to challenge the slowest member of the opposition to what was generously termed a 'sprint'. Boosted by victory over his even less athletic Auckland team-mate Aaron Barnes – a race which persuaded Richardson to take the challenge to the Test arena – he surprised onlookers by outpacing Pakistan's Danish Kaneria over 100m on Boxing Day 2003, only to be beaten by South Africa's Neil McKenzie three months later. 'The South Africans really struggled to understand the principle of the whole thing,' complained Richardson, who suspected that McKenzie was actually their hare rather than their tortoise. 'They're very competitive and they took it a bit seriously.'

Once Richardson had calmed down, England's Ashley Giles pipped him on the line at Trent Bridge in 2004, before Australia's Darren Lehmann was left for dead at the Adelaide Oval. By this stage Richardson was wearing an emetic beige-and-brown Lycra outfit given to him by the New Zealand supporters club, the BEIGE BRIGADE. 'It didn't leave much to the imagination,' said one local journalist, gagging slightly. His final appearance came in February 2006, over a year after his retirement, when he agreed to a four-man sprint at Auckland, where New

Zealand were playing a TWENTY20 international against West Indies. Showing a worrying aptitude for the event, Richardson was beaten only by the Auckland Blues RUGBY player Jerome Kaino, and left Anna Lawrence (the former captain of New Zealand's hockey team) and Tony Veitch (a sports presenter) in his wake. Exhausted by it all, he was expected to arrive home some time in 2009.

See also SUPERSTITION.

SLOWER BALL

If variety is the spice of life, then the slower ball is cricket's salt and pepper – the first and most obvious variation employed by SEAM bowlers to keep the batsmen guessing. Executed well, of course, the slower ball is not obvious at all, and batsmen who fail to spot it can end up playing about three shots before it reaches them, each one more panicky than the last. Worse, they can end up being greeted with tabloid headlines such as 'Silly Ducker!' – which is what happened to England's Chris Read when he tried to avoid what he thought was a BEAMER from Chris Cairns of New Zealand during the LORD's Test in 1999. In fact, Cairns had produced the perfect slower ball and ended up hitting the stumps with a YORKER as Read cowered for his life. After the end of the series, Read did not play another Test for four years.

Cairns's sleight of hand typifies the way in which the slower ball has gradually become a weapon in its own right rather than a last resort. 'When Ian Botham tried one at Taunton,' wrote Frank Keating in the *Guardian* not long after Cairns had foxed Read, 'you could unfailingly spot it from Yeovil.' Cairns honed the art while he was playing for Nottinghamshire, where the West Indian Franklyn Stephenson was the past-master of the craft. In 1988, Stephenson claimed 125 wickets for the county, and reckoned that a quarter of them came courtesy of the slower one. Since then, experts have included Courtney Walsh, who made a mug of Graham Thorpe in 2000; the Australia one-day specialist Ian Harvey, whose slower ball could have broken into Fort Knox; and the former Surrey and England one-day captain Adam Hollioake, who duped countless county batsmen with a knuckle ball borrowed from baseball, where the ball perches on the knuckles of the middle and ring fingers.

The Hollioake variation was one of many. Harvey preferred to release his slower ball from out of the back of the hand, while others – such as Darren Gough and Shoaib Akhtar – essentially bowl disguised OFF-BREAKS. It might not be manly, which is probably why the slower ball took years to cotton on, but it sure is effective. And as a means of deflating a batsman's ego, it comes second only to yanking his trousers down mid-pitch.

SNICKOMETER

When Channel 4 began televising England's home Tests in 1999, one of the many gadgets they employed to make the old BBC coverage look as lively as one of their early-morning Open University broadcasts was the snickometer. The brainchild of Alan Plaskett, the snicko – yes, cricket loves its nicknames – picked up the faintest of sounds via the stump and pitch microphones, and conveyed its findings to the viewer in the form of a Richter scale-like monitor. If the sound-frequency pattern is disturbed, causing a minor tremor, then it indicates the ball hit something. If the pattern does not move at all, then the bowler is either appealing mistakenly or, more likely, trying to pull a fast one on the 67-year-old umpire with the ear trumpet.

Problems arise, of course, when it is unclear what has caused the sound. Since a tremor can be triggered by ball on bat, ball on pad, bat on pad, or – in the case of Inzamam-ul-Haq – the rumblings of the stomach, the evidence is not always conclusive, which is probably why the authorities have so far resisted calls to make the snickometer official. But they did experiment during the 2004 ICC Champions Trophy in England by wiring umpires up to the stump microphones to help with contentious appeals for caught behind. Umpires said it made little or no difference, but in May 2006 the ICC recommended earpieces for the umpires in all international matches.

Until then, the men in white had been left to incur the wrath of the armchair expert, who had access to the snickometer's – mainly unambiguous – data and hurled know-it-all abuse at the TV when the sound of a thin edge failed to carry 22 yards to the umpire above 100,000 screaming fans in Kolkata. Apologists for this sorry state of affairs harped on about the romanticism of human error, as if incorrectly giving Sachin Tendulkar not out on 0 in Lahore was a laughing matter.

See also ANALYST, THE; HAWKEYE; NICK.

SQUARE

The collection of pitches in the middle of a cricket ground, only one of which will be in use at any given time. Groundsmen protect the square as if it is their only child, and no game these days is complete without a solemn warning from the PA announcer to 'keep off the square'. A phalanx of orange-jacketed heavies surrounding it at the end of a match proves just how important the square really is. It's an area of the pitch batsmen don't like being associated with either. If they are struggling with their timing, they are often said to be unable to 'get the ball off the square', an insult which doubles up by implying utter feebleness too.

See also CORDON; STREAKERS.

STICKY WICKET

These days, to be trapped on a sticky wicket is to be part of one of cricket's most ghastly clichés. But there was a time when it meant a lot more than that. In the days when cricket pitches were left uncovered, and thus at the mercy of the weather, sticky wickets would come about as the sun dried out a sodden pitch. The result was a spin bowler's paradise, as the pitch – soft and yielding below a thin, dry crust – misbehaved like a Premiership FOOT-BALLER on a night out.

With its mixture of tropical storms and sweltering heat, Brisbane produced some of the stickiest wickets – or sticky dogs, as the locals called it – in the business. During the 1950–51 ASHES Test there, RAIN turned the third-day pitch into a lottery: England DECLARED at 68 for 7 in an attempt to force Australia to bat in the unplayable conditions, only for Australia to end their second innings on 32 for 7 and then reduce England to 30 for 6 by the close.

Listen to former players and you would think that uncovered pitches were not simply a way of engendering better batting techniques, but a cure for old age and the solution to world peace. The modern fan just reckons they made ordinary bowlers look better than they really were. Whatever the truth, the sticky wicket remains the hassled headline-writer's dream.

STOCK BALL

The ball that forms the majority of a bowler's repertoire, like Anil Kumble's TOP-SPINNER, Matthew Hoggard's away-SWINGER, and Devon Malcolm's leg-stump HALF-VOLLEY.

See also RADAR.

STONEWALL

The *Oxford English Dictionary* defines the verb 'to stonewall' – in cricketing terms, at least – as 'to bat with excessive caution'. But this merely hints at the sense-numbing bloody-mindedness of the archetypal stone-waller, a batsman who derives perverse pleasure from blocking the bejesus out of the ball and then claims he was doing it in the interests of his team-mates. Since most of them will by now be fast asleep, this explanation is rarely convincing.

And yet the stonewaller can always point to his natural place in a game which can last up to five days and still end in a draw. Why else would *WISDEN* devote a separate table to 'Slowest Individual Batting'? The list gives rise to some interesting insights. Of the twenty-two innings included in the 2006 edition, six were played by Englishmen (whose batsmen have, as often as not, been performing with their backs to the wall), and five each by New Zealanders (the spiritual home of the stonewaller) and Pakistanis (where the slowness of the pitches breeds either risk-takers or careful accumulators). Australia and West Indies, traditionally the two most attack-minded Test nations, have no entrants.

Top of the list is the New Zealand No. 11 Geoff Allott, who in 101 minutes of almost unadulterated forward defensives against South Africa at Auckland in March 1999 scored precisely no runs. 'It was the best DUCK I'll ever make,' he grinned afterwards. At least Allott's go-slow made sense. During the opening match of the inaugural World Cup in 1975, India's Sunil Gavaskar set about the task of chasing down England's massive 334 for 4 from 60 overs. He batted throughout the Indian reply, by which time he had advanced to an utterly mystifying 36 from 174 balls, an innings of such staggering selfishness that India finished on 132 for 3. He later explained that since he believed India had no chance of scoring the runs he had opted for batting practice instead. In a touching show of solidarity, a spectator then opted for *target* practice by dumping his LUNCH at Gavaskar's feet.

But Allott and Gavaskar merely stonewalled for a day. Some batsmen did it for an entire career. One of them, Geoff Boycott, was famously run out by his own team-mate Ian Botham because he had spent two hours making 26 runs at Wellington. The fact that Boycott was captain at the time made the decision even more mutinous, but since England went on to win the game it was also justified. Another, Ken Mackay, was such an oddity – an Australian who was content to defend – that he earned the nickname 'Slasher'.

But research by CRICINFO in 2005 revealed that the most painstaking stonewaller among batsmen who had scored 1,000 Test runs was the England wicketkeeper Bob Taylor, who crept along at a rate of 27.13 runs per 100 balls during his 57-match career. The second and third names on the list – Mike Brearley (29.79) and Chris Tavaré (30.60) – are also Englishmen, a fact which might encourage Australian readers to draw their own conclusions.

See also MASTER, THE; NETS; STRIKE-RATE; WILLOW.

STREAKERS

The thrill you get from shedding your clothes and hurdling the stumps must be a bit like the frisson derived from burping in front of great aunt Maud: it's the look on everyone's faces that counts, especially in the press box, where initial murmurs of disapproval are immediately followed by a mad rush for the binoculars. This is probably why cricket, with its pretensions to gentility, attracts more streakers than most.

Sport's most celebrated exhibitionist is Erica Roe, who nearly knocked a policeman out with her assets during a RUGBY international between England and Australia at Twickenham in 1982. But cricket had got there first. The first example of a streaker at a FIRST-CLASS cricket match took place during the ASHES Test at LORD'S in 1975, when a cook in the Merchant Navy calling himself Michael Angelow was fined £20 for his troubles. 'It's a freaker!' enthused Trevor Bailey on *TEST MATCH SPECIAL*. His co-commentator John Arlott was more measured. 'Not very shapely,' he noted dryly. 'And it's masculine. He's now being marched in a final exhibition past at least 8,000 people in the Mound Stand, some of whom, perhaps, have never seen anything quite like this before.'

Since then, the nudists have threatened to take over the asylum on a regular basis. During the Old Trafford Test between England and West Indies in August 2000, there were four such invasions, prompting Nasser Hussain to lament: 'It gets you down a little bit if people think it's more entertaining to run on the pitch with no clothes on.' These days streakers receive far more than a clip round the ear from a grinning bobby: a charge of aggravated trespass awaits.

But the exhibitionists are cleverer than that. Two New Zealand women caused a stir during a one-day international in January 2006 at the far-from-racy venue of McLean Park in Napier when their kiss was caught on the giant screen. A security guard muscled over to put a stop to the nonsense, which did not please the snoggers. 'I doubt it would have distracted the players,' said Richelle Fitzgibbon, a 29-year-old mother of three. 'I wouldn't kiss an unattractive girl – I do draw the line.'

See also CHOCOLATE CAKE.

STRIKE-RATE

For batsmen, the number of runs scored per 100 balls; for bowlers, the number of balls delivered per wicket. To generalize gratuitously, a very good batting strike-rate in Test cricket would be anything over 55; bowlers aim for anything under. Australia's Adam Gilchrist raised the bar to Olympic high-jump proportions with his strike-rate of 81.59 (as at 20 April 2006), while Pakistan's Waqar Younis struck once every 47.95 balls, the best of the moderns.

STUMPS

The notion that the three stumps (28 inches high and 9 across) do little more than sit at both ends of the pitch and wait to be hit by a bowler or a fielder was shown to be mistaken during the final of India's Duleep Trophy at Jamshedpur in January 1991. An ongoing tiff between the North Zone opener Raman Lamba and the West Zone bowler Rashid Patel came to a head when Patel treated Lamba to a BEAMER. Enraged, Lamba advanced towards Patel brandishing his bat, to which Patel's response was to grab a stump in what he later described as self-defence (it was a gesture which lent a different perspective to the umpire's traditional call of 'stumps' after the last ball of the day has been delivered). Their mid-pitch battle – 'the most shameful moment in the history of Indian cricket', according to WISDEN – sparked a riot in the crowd and brought an ill-tempered match to a merciful draw. Patel was banned for thirteen months, and Lamba for ten, but there was to be a tragic postscript. Seven years later Lamba, whose brief international career had already come and gone by the time he fenced with Patel, was hit on his helmetless head while fielding at short leg during a club match in Bangladesh. He died in hospital three days later.

See also FIELDING POSITIONS; HELMET; WICKET.

SUPER SERIES

Don't be fooled. This was a series that was not so much super as superfluous. As with most bad cricket concepts, it concerned money. The ICC decided it would be a good idea for the best team in the world to take on the rest in three one-day internationals and a six-day Super Test in October 2005. There were three problems: the best team in the world was Australia, who had just had their status called into question by losing to England; the World XI did not give a hoot; and the six-day Test match turned into a three-and-a-bit-day mismatch. Not surprisingly, Australia won all four games at a canter, while members of the World XI – when they weren't squabbling about who was going to field at first slip – let it be known that they found the whole concept as inspiring as a wet Wednesday in Derby. By the end, even the ICC were doubting the wisdom of repeating the event. Yes, it was that bad.

See also SHOCKER.

SUPERSTITION

Sportsmen don't come any more superstitious than cricketers, which is no surprise when some of them have little more to do than sit around in the pavilion all day waiting to bat and mulling over the prospect of another DUCK. No wonder the mind starts to play more tricks than Darren Gough let loose with a pair of scissors in a sock shop. Superstitions like NELSON (111, 222, etc.) and the Devil's Number (87) are well-known, but it is the more obscure personal foibles ('Must remember to put left pad on first!') which might persuade you to inch quietly towards the door.

The idea that we can influence our performance on the pitch with anything other than runs, wickets, catches and a cool head is ingrained in the average player. So much so that the *Cricketers' Who's Who*, the frighteningly thorough annual guide to FIRST-CLASS players in the UK, thinks nothing of asking the cream of the nation's crop to name their 'cricket superstitions'. Lumped together, the answers amount to a smorgasbord of eccentricity, plus several dollops of chaos theory left to go funny in the sun.

James Averis says he always uses the same toilet, which presumably proves problematic when Gloucestershire are not playing at home. Michael Brown of Hampshire insists on tapping the non-striker's end four times with his bat after every over (but only if he finishes the over at that end, of course). Whenever Surrey's Mark Ramprakash is not out overnight, he will take the piece of gum he was chewing, stick it on the end of his bat handle, and – probably best not to try this one at home – continue chewing it the next morning. Hampshire's Greek-South African wicketkeeper, Nic Pothas, says he has 'too many to mention'. Anyone who has seen him perform his repertoire of carefully calibrated gestures at the CREASE between balls will agree.

The former England wicketkeeper Jack Russell had a whole range of bizarre mannerisms, which explained why the subtitle of his autobiography was *Barking?*. Match-day LUNCHES consisted of Weetabix which had been left to soak in milk for precisely eight minutes, 'so that their consistency,' as his former captain Mike Atherton wrote, 'was soft but not mushy'. He would use the same TEA-bag for an entire Test match, hanging it on a peg for inter-cuppa breathers. And he has claimed he wants his hands amputated and preserved in formaldehyde after his death. Yikes.

But Russell is pushed all the way by South Africa's Neil McKenzie, who was good enough to win forty-one Test caps as a middle-order batsman. The question is: how many more would he have won had he not been such a bundle of tics and affectations? McKenzie transposed the old worry about treading on cracks in the pavement on to the cricket field, where he was ultra-careful not to stand on any white lines, and was regularly teased by the Australians if he ever came close. And if it wasn't one thing it was another: every single toilet seat in the dressing-room had to be down while he was out in the middle.

One story reveals McKenzie's quirks better than any other. His team-mate Mark Boucher remembers McKenzie dragging his equipment up several flights of stairs to the dressing-room, where Boucher opened the bag and picked up one of the bats. Big mistake: no one touched McKenzie's bats before McKenzie himself. So he lugged his kit back down the stairs, put it back in the team bus and then did the whole thing all over again. Ridiculous, really. Now, about that four-leaf clover . . .

See also COFFIN; SLOWCOACH.

SUPERSUB

At 1.02pm on Thursday, 7 July 2005, at Headingley in Leeds, England's Vikram Solanki became the world's first supersub – a name which, like those tabloid FOOTBALL-transfer stories that miraculously appear in five different papers under the word 'exclusive', is less honest than it would like to be. The sub bit is fine; it's the super that most people had problems with.

The concept, dreamed up by the ICC on what was presumably one of their quieter days, derived from the noble enough intention of spicing up the 50-overs-a-side one-day international following the impact of TWENTY20.

It allowed both sides to replace one member of their team at any stage of the game with their designated supersub, who could then do whatever the player he had replaced had not yet done. Solanki, for example, replaced Simon Jones after thirty-one overs of Australia's innings, by which time Jones had bowled his allocation of ten. That meant that, although Solanki could not now bowl, he could replace Jones in the batting order when England came to chase down Australia's total (while Jones could take no further part in the game). In the event Solanki was not needed because England won by nine wickets, but the new rule had in theory given them an extra option.

So far, so so. But there was one major flaw, and that's aside from the obvious objection that twelve-a-side cricket makes fewer demands on the captain and thus dilutes the need for tactical ingenuity. The main problem was that the supersub had to be named *before* the TOSS had taken place, which handed an unfair advantage to the team who called correctly. Captains and coaches pleaded for a change to the rules so that the supersubs could be nominated *after* the toss instead. After much ridicule, the ICC went even further than that and at a meeting in February 2006, at the end of its ten-month trial period, recommended that the rule be scrapped altogether. While the world waited for the recommendation to be put into practice, South Africa and Australia took the law into their own hands ahead of their five-match one-day series by agreeing not to use supersubs at all.

SWEEP

The sweep treads a ridiculously fine line between ingenuity and incompetence, and as such suffers the same fate as most leg-side strokes. Get it right, as Graham Gooch did during England's 1987 World Cup semi-final win over India, and the commentators will praise its capacity to disrupt; get it wrong, as four England batsmen contrived to do on the first day of the Lahore Test in November 2005, and they question the batsmen's sanity, moral rectitude and suitability to father children, let alone play international cricket. Played on one knee in the knowledge that the ball could easily hit you in the face, the sweep is hard enough to execute without these repercussions to consider.

Like a *News of the World* journalist/sheikh, the sweep is a many-faced creature. The most conventional version ends up at deep-backward square leg and earns the batsman a single. But there is also the sweep aimed straighter through square leg, as exhibited by Australia's Matthew Hayden during his run-laden tour of India in 2001. There is the paddle sweep, played with an almost vertical bat, *à la* Nasser Hussain. There is the SLOG-sweep, fetched from outside off-stump, which Hansie Cronje and Steve Waugh mastered to make conventional off-spinners look like cannon fodder. There is the scoop, which was briefly perfected by Zimbabwe's Doug Marillier, involves helping the ball over the right-handed batsman's left shoulder, and almost deserves a category of its own. And then there was John Emburey's unique falling-over sweep, which scored more highly for efficiency than it did for style. The former England wicketkeeper Alan Knott could sweep almost anything, while Lancashire's Mal Loye developed an insane but thrilling piece of premeditation in which he swept the fast bowlers high over midwicket for six, while keeping his dentist interested at the same time.

And then, of course, there is the reverse-sweep, a shot

which gained notoriety when Mike Gatting got out to it at a crucial stage of the 1987 World Cup final against Australia. England went on to lose the game by 7 runs and the stroke became as popular as the poll tax. The chairman of selectors, Peter May, reflected the public's outrage by virtually banning it, and for years it was the shot that dared not speak its name.

In fact, the reverse-sweep had been used to great effect by Pakistan's Mushtaq Mohammad as early as 1970, and there is even a reference in the 1920s to Duleepsinhji playing a delivery 'backwards towards third man with his bat turned and facing the wicketkeeper'. According to L. P. Jai, the batsman at the other end, 'there was an appeal for unfair play but the umpire ruled it out.' Post-Gatting, however, it was not until Warwickshire began to demonstrate the stroke's field-scattering ability in the mid-1990s that its reputation as a totem of evil lessened. Zimbabwe's Andy Flower regarded it as a genuine run-scoring option, and New Zealand's Craig McMillan even switched hands on the bat handle, which raised questions about the lbw Law. Had McMillan turned himself into a left-hander mid-stroke? If so, was his off-stump now his leg-stump? And did that affect the umpire's decision about where the ball pitched? There have been times when you get the feeling some people wish the reverse-sweep had never happened.

See also FIELDING POSITIONS; HOOK; LEG BEFORE WICKET; PULL.

SWING

One of the great mysteries of the game, along with Saqlain Mushtaq's DOOSRA and the Test career of Ronnie Irani.

No one has satisfactorily explained why the ball should move in the air, although there are plenty of theories, including the amount of moisture in the atmosphere, the make of the ball, and the vigour with which the man at mid-off has been sucking sweets and coating the ball with sugared saliva – a crime which once cost India's Rahul Dravid half his match fee. The most common explanation is that the shiny side of the ball (this is why bowlers spend so much time rubbing it on their inner thigh – OK, their groin) travels more quickly through the air than the side that is left to go rough. But swing is such an elusive quality that generalities seem pointless.

Reverse-swing is even harder to pigeon-hole. The position of the SEAM does not change (it still points towards first slip, as per the conventional away-swinger to the right-handed batsman), but – as if by magic! – the ball swings the other way. Reverse-swing experts, like the Pakistanis and more recently the English, aim to keep one side of the ball as dry as possible and it is thought that this drier, rougher side eventually becomes lighter than the side which has been kept shiny. Perhaps because they don't like the thought that the English reverse the ball better than they do, the Australians refer to the phenomenon as 'Irish'.

One thing is certain: when a swing bowler gets it right, he can be unstoppable. On his Test debut at LORD'S in June 1972, Australia's Bob Massie made the ball look like a boomerang on his way to match figures of 16 for 137, but – as the luck of the Irish deserted him – he managed just fifteen wickets in his next five Tests before being dropped for good.

See also ASHES, THE; BALL-TAMPERING.

TAIL

The collective name given to lower-order batsmen, or tail-enders, or 'nine, ten, jack' as the old-timers prefer it. If the tail does well, it is said to 'wag'. If it doesn't, then RABBIT imagery becomes even more appropriate, since a rabbit's tail is, frankly, hardly worthy of the name.

See also DUCK; FERRET.

TAPEBALL

One of the many ways in which Pakistanis like to irritate Indians is by pointing out that most of the subcontinent's greatest fast bowlers have come from west of the post-Partition border. And one of the reasons usually given for this imbalance is the street game of tapeball. At first, this sounds like putting France's victory in the 1998 World Cup down to their passion for table FOOTBALL, but tapeball is no bistro *divertissement*. Wrap a tennis ball in tape (the proper brown stuff, not sellotape) and leave a little slit on one side. Then change into your cricket gear, carefully ensuring the pin on your Blue Peter badge is not about to take someone's eye out, and bowl as fast as you can. The weight imbalance caused by the slit should help the ball to SWING, leaving you feeling like Wasim Akram and the batsman looking like Courtney Walsh. Ever since the 1980s, Pakistani boys have grown up with tapeball, and a favourite theory is that the extra effort needed to propel the lighter ball from one wicket (or dustbin) to another helps build muscles, which in turn helps create meaner, leaner fast bowlers. Their only surprise is that their arch-rivals have not yet cottoned on. In *Pundits from Pakistan* Rahul Bhattacharya, an Indian journalist, is so taken with tapeball that he can't stop talking about it. Eventually, a Pakistani colleague turns to him and says: 'Wait a minute, you mean you have *no* tapeball cricket in India?' Bhattacharya nods. 'Oh,' says the Pakistani, in what might well have been a mixture of surprise, pity, and disdain.

See also DUCK; JOURNALISM.

TEA

In *Asterix in Britain* the invading Romans are nonplussed by the natives' habit of breaking off hostilities for some hot water with a 'spot of milk'. Cricket has ensured that this bizarre tradition lives on. The tea break is even more of an indulgence than LUNCH, which at least helps satisfy the human need for three square meals a day. Yet a common complaint in the annual *Cricketers' Who's Who* is that tea should be longer than the twenty minutes normally set aside. And to think the average English county pro is regarded by his Australian counterpart as a skiver . . .

Cricket teas, though, are more than a paper plateful of cheese-and-pickle sandwiches and a fairy cake. They are part of the warp and weft of English society, at least if the well-heeled readers of *Country Life* magazine are to be believed. Responding in a poll to the question 'Which of the following most embodies the British summer?', a not inconsiderable 9 per cent voted for 'cricket teas', which placed them joint-fourth in a list of ten, behind only tennis at Wimbledon (30 per cent), Pimm's at sundown (20 per cent), and village fetes (15 per cent). But since the same questionnaire revealed that 30 per cent of readers regarded hunting as their favourite pastime, perhaps this is not a reason for celebration.

The most famous teas on the county circuit can be found at New Road in Worcestershire, where the social status of the tea ladies – they have, after all, been serving up fruit loaves and cheese scones in the Ladies' Pavilion since 1970 – is reflected by the fact that they have their own spaces in the club car park.

But not all ladies regard baking cakes for their men as a natural part of society's evolution. For some, the art of creating the perfect crust has been nothing less than a catalyst for revolution. In November 2005 five female members of Oldham Cricket Club became the first WOMEN to attend the annual Central Lancashire League dinner since it began in 1892. One of them, Kath Inkpen, told the *Oldham Advertiser*: 'Women are just expected to do the cricket teas and that's it. We got a few strange looks from people who weren't expecting us there – but it was a very good night.' The League chairman, Mr Howard Dronsfield, noted that the 'language was quite strong but the ladies all enjoyed themselves'. At future dinners, they might even be allowed to join in with the swearing.

TEAPOT

The *sine qua non* of the TEA-break. Also the pose adopted by a disgruntled captain, hands on hips, when his leading fast bowler serves up a leg-stump HALF-VOLLEY moments after the fielder at midwicket has been moved to fifth slip. This relationship was perfected by Graham Gooch and his dangerous but unpredictable fast bowler Devon Malcolm.

See also RADAR; STOCK BALL.

TEBBIT TEST

It's not that sport and politics don't mix. It's just that they tend not to mix very well. Just ask Norman Tebbit, the former chairman of the Conservative Party. During an interview with the *Los Angeles Times* in 1990, Tebbit noted: 'A large proportion of Britain's Asian population fail to pass the cricket test. Which side do they cheer for? It's an interesting test. Are you still harking back to where you came from or where you are?' Tebbit's crude attempt to categorize the allegiances of second- and third-generation Asian immigrants was never forgotten, not least by the man himself. After four suicide bombers – three of Pakistani origin, one from Jamaica – killed fifty-two London commuters on 7 July 2005, Tebbit told the website ePolitix.com: 'I do think had my comments been acted on those attacks would have been less likely. What I was saying about the so-called cricket test is that it was a test of whether a community has integrated. If a community was looking back at where it had come from instead of looking forward with the people to whom they had come to then there is going to be a problem sooner or later.'

Cricket itself has largely steered clear of the Tebbit test, although the Indian-born Nasser Hussain caused a stir in 2001 when he called upon young British Asians to support

England rather the country of their parents and grand-parents. A quick strawpoll during that summer's Old Trafford Test against Pakistan revealed that Hussain was fighting a losing battle. 'We'd have appreciated it from Usman Afzaal or Owais Shah – one of the Asians on the county circuit – but not from Nasser,' said a 28-year-old Anglo-Asian in the crowd. 'We regard him as 100 per cent English. We even used to think he was half-Cypriot or something.'

TEST

The important thing here is the upper-case T. Test cricket is no mere test. It is, as we are repeatedly told, a Test, mainly because it lasts five days and thus tests the patience of batsmen, bowlers and terrestrial broadcasters who are concerned about eating into the air-time of the latest edition of *Hollyoaks*.

The first Test took place at Melbourne in March 1877, when Australia beat England by 45 runs, thanks mainly to an innings of 165 (retired hurt) out of 245 from the Kent-born Charles Bannerman. At the time of writing, no one had passed Bannerman's figure of 69.6 per cent of his side's runs off the bat. Just as improbably, when the two sides met in the Centenary Test at the same venue 100 years later, the result was exactly the same: a win for Australia by 45 runs. The third Test between England and Sri Lanka at Trent Bridge in June 2006 was the 1,804th since Bannerman laid down his marker.

See also QUEEN, THE; TIMELESS TESTS; TWENTY20.

Back in 1993, while the rest of the world was coming to grips with the war in Yugoslavia and the Israeli–Palestine peace accord, the cricket-loving Prime Minister, John Major, was outlining his grand vision of the future. 'Fifty years from now,' he declared, 'Britain will still be the country of long shadows on county grounds, warm beer, invincible green suburbs, dog lovers and pool fillers and – as George Orwell said – "old maids cycling to Holy Communion through the morning mist".' BBC Radio's *Test Match Special* (198 LW) is as close as sports broadcasting has come to upholding that peculiarly nostalgic form of Britishness. The commentators chat about pigeons and buses, scoff CHOCOLATE CAKES sent in by the Tunbridge Wells Women's Institute, and call each other by nicknames straight out of boarding school. Needless to say, the nation loves them.

The BBC began ball-by-ball radio coverage in 1957, since when no summer has felt entirely complete without the likes of Brian Johnston, Jonathan Agnew, Henry Blofeld and Bill Frindall (that's Johnners, Aggers, Blowers and Bearders to you). The quality of the banter is such that cricket devotees have often watched coverage of the cricket with the sound on their TVs turned down and the radio turned up, but it is the eccentricities which appeal as much as anything. Blofeld calls everyone 'my dear old thing', which probably disguises the fact he has forgotten their names. Bill 'Bearded Wonder' Frindall, the scorer, harrumphs from the back of the box when anyone gets a statistic wrong. And Agnew keeps the whole thing going with his infectious enthusiasm.

John Arlott used to lend a sense of gravitas with his

rich south-coast vowels – invariably described as a 'Hampshire burr' – but after he retired to a standing ovation from the LORD's crowd and the Australian fielders during the Centenary Test in 1980, the mood became more light-hearted. It's doubtful whether any other radio programme could have got away with several minutes of bent-double giggling from Johnston and Agnew following a reference to Ian Botham's failure to 'get his leg over' after he was out hit wicket against West Indies in 1991. But *TMS* did, and the excerpt passed into broadcasting legend. Not even the interruptions of the shipping forecast, which turned North Sea outposts such as Cromarty, Forties and Viking into household names to rival Botham, Richards and Lillee, have put listeners off.

See also DISMISSALS; JOURNALISM; STREAKERS.

THREE MEN (AND A DOG)

The average attendance at a county championship match – if you choose to take at face value those misleading photographs which focus on a lone OAP sipping from a Thermos. Of course, the reality is not quite as bad as that (heck, the dog often brings a friend), but before cricket became cool in 2005 the pensioner shot was an easy way for newspaper sports editors to kick off their coverage of the season in wet and windy April. The counties, though, have not always helped themselves, and there have been times when it has been tricky to disagree with Bob Willis's DISMISSAL of followers of the domestic game as a bunch of social misfits and trainspotters. (A rash attempt to alter perceptions took place at Worcester after a one-day game in July 1997, when six spectators from Cardiff were becalmed by CS spray and arrested after one of them punched a policeman.) A rumour once circulated that only three paying customers had entered Leicestershire's Grace Road for a day of championship cricket, but all three disappeared before it could be corroborated. Meanwhile Derbyshire, always the first butt of jokes about county cricket, sold cheap memberships to dogs, a scheme they abandoned when the dogs lost interest. TWENTY20 has revolutionized the way county cricket is perceived, but getting bums on seats in the longer form of the game remains a struggle, and the members who do turn up on a regular basis are generally referred to as 'hardy perennials'. That's to their faces, mind . . .

See also TREADMILL.

TIE

A tie occurs in a four-innings match when the side batting last is dismissed for one run fewer than the total it was chasing for victory – in other words, when both sides' totals add up to exactly the same (in one-day matches, ties take place when both teams finish with the same score, although sometimes the number of wickets lost is used as a tie-breaker). There have been two ties in Test cricket: at Brisbane in December 1960, when not even all of the Australian and West Indian players were sure of the result after Joe Solomon's direct hit from square-leg ran out Ian Meckiff; and at Madras in September 1986, when Australia's Greg Matthews trapped India's No. 11 Maninder Singh lbw for a DUCK. Only once in Test cricket has a game ended as a draw with the scores level, when England, set 205, finished on 204 for 6 against Zimbabwe at Bulawayo in December 1996. It was a result which prompted the England coach David Lloyd to tell the press 'We flippin' murdered 'em.' Unfortunately, England had merely drawn with 'em.

See also BENAUD, RICHIE; CHUCKING; ONE-DAY INTERNATIONAL.

TIMELESS TESTS

Watching a timeless Test that runs out of time must be like ordering a steak-and-kidney pie without the steak or kidney. Or the pie. Yet this is precisely what happened at Durban in March 1939, in the days when Tests were some-times played to a finish, regardless of the number of spectators who had to be woken up every evening at stumps. South Africa had set Wally Hammond's England a near-impossible 696 to win the fifth and final Test and secure a 2–0 series win. But when RAIN began to fall around TEA-time on the tenth – yes, tenth – day of the match, they had reached a scarcely credible 654 for 5, thanks in part to a local rule which allowed the pitch to be repaired at the end of each day's play.

The only problem was that the England players had a ship to catch, and the ship in question, the *Athlone Castle*, was straining at the anchor in Cape Town. So instead of hanging around for one more day to complete one of the most famous wins in the history of Test cricket, the England team decided to catch a train that night, call it a draw and head for home. The 1,981 runs scored in that match remain a world record, but it was not enough to save the concept of the timeless Test, which was con-veniently forgotten about after the war and is these days regarded with a bemused fondness, like tea cosies or Cannon and Ball. About sixty years later, Steve Waugh proposed the abolition of the fifth day, mainly because his Australia side were beating everyone else in four. Which means that he would probably have been able to fit three whole victories into the twelve days (nine on the field, one dodging the rain, and two taking a breather) required by South Africa and England in 1939.

TOP-SPINNER

Imagine Andy Murray passing Roger Federer at the net with a cross-court forehand played with top-spin, and visualize the extra kick in the tennis ball after it bounces. LEG-BREAK bowlers strive for the same effect when they deliver their own top-spinner (bowled with the back of the hand facing up, then towards the batsman): the ball will go straight on but should surprise the batsman with its bounce. India's Anil Kumble, who in February 1999 against Pakistan at Delhi became only the second player after Jim Laker to take all ten wickets in a Test innings, is usually described as a leg-spinner, but bowls mainly top-spinners. This probably explains the following assessment from the former England coach Keith Fletcher, out in Johannesburg on a spying mission ahead of his side's tour of India in 1992–93: 'I didn't see him TURN a single ball from leg to off. I don't believe we will have much problem with him.' Shortly afterwards, Kumble took 21 English wickets at less than 20 apiece and India won 3–0.

See also FLIPPER; GOOGLY; ZOOTER.

TOSS

W. G. GRACE had the right idea. Rather than waste time uttering 'heads' or 'tails', he was once said to have dispensed with the toss altogether and marched out with his brother Edward to open the batting before his opposite number knew what was going on. Those captains who do turn up for the toss, and end up winning it, usually decide that batting first is a good idea, although research by a Melbourne academic in 2004 questioned this cherished notion. Professor Stephen Clarke analysed the results of 151 Tests played between 1997 and 2001 and found that the side batting second won 49 per cent of matches, compared with only 26 per cent by the side batting first.

But the news came too late for Pakistan's Salim Malik. When his side met Zimbabwe at Harare in January 1995, Malik called 'birds' rather than 'heads', in recognition of the national symbol on the local coins. Zimbabwe's captain, Andy Flower, had already conceded defeat when the match referee, Jackie Hendriks, complained that he had not heard the call. Predictably, the re-toss was won by Flower, who chose to bat first and duly hit 156 in his side's total of 544 for 4. Pakistan were then dismissed for 322 and 158 to hand Zimbabwe their first victory in Test cricket. Cue lame gags about Malik being a useless tosser . . .

See also MATCH-FIXING.

TRAVOLTA, JOHN (1954–)

It's fair to say that John Travolta has never strutted his stuff in Derbyshire's County Ground (it's just off the

Pentagon Island roundabout, John, where the A61 meets the A52), but that didn't stop him injuring the county's star ALL-ROUNDER in July 2004. Graeme Welch was listening to a *Grease* CD in the car and teaching his son Ethan the moves when Welch Jnr poked his dad in the eye. To add injury to injury, Ethan had recently stopped biting his nails, thus turning his Travolta impression into a lethal weapon and forcing Graeme to miss Derbyshire's next game. The eye-patch he had to wear did little to assuage the sheepishness. Just as bizarrely, Travolta is also the middle name of David Mutendera, the right-arm seamer who played one Test and nine one-day internationals for Zimbabwe.

See also SHOCKER.

TREADMILL

The treadmill vies with the bar as the place you are most likely to find county cricketers in the local Trusthouse Forte (although in April 1999 Glamorgan's seventeen-year-old seamer David Harrison was not allowed to use the gym at his team's hotel in Derby without adult supervision). The treadmill is also an apt metaphor for the *ennui* of the county journeyman, forever condemned to head down the M1 for a game in Leicester minutes after finishing one in Nottingham and four days before starting another in Northampton.

In fact, the county treadmill is often the most convenient scapegoat for the failings of the national side, an argument that begins to fray at the edges when overseas pros praise England's domestic structure for providing them with the chance to hone their game, to say nothing of their knowledge of the British motorway network.

TURN

What spinners hope the ball will do once it has hit the pitch. An unwritten rule of cricket writing states that turn is always 'extracted', as if it were a troublesome molar; usually 'sharp'; and often accompanied by the words 'and bounce'. English spinners regard turn as something of a holy grail. Non-English spinners regard it simply as the basis for negotiation.

TWENTY20

If Test cricket is a finger-licking three-course dinner plus coffee, mints, and a post-prandial snooze, and the 50-over game a microwave lasagne with ready-made salad, then what contrived culinary metaphor can we find for Twenty20? A pot noodle? Or a bag of prawn cocktail? In fact, the newest arrival on cricket's menu has proved far more substantial than that. In April 2002 the English cricket establishment reacted to falling attendances in the county championship by approving the introduction of a new form of the game to attract a new audience. In 2003, Twenty20 took the shires by storm, and provided a gift-wrapped excuse for grateful journalists to make puns about perfect vision. Fans flocked in their thousands; women and children were spotted. County cricket was in danger of becoming cool.

The competition's popularity grew over the next two seasons as the public lapped up the benefits of a game that took place after work and lasted only 2¾ hours. It even spread beyond the domestic arena, although the decision by the New Zealand players to grow comedy facial HAIR for the inaugural Twenty20 international against Australia in Auckland in February 2005 suggested that not everyone was taking it seriously (New Zealand looked even sillier when they lost by 44 runs).

Critics argued that it wasn't proper cricket – 'hit-and-giggle' was the favourite term of abuse – but the voices of dissent were lost in a sea of praise, and most observers began to cast a critical eye over the 50-over game, with its identikit middle overs when batsmen MILKED spinners for singles. Since Twenty20 distilled the best bits of the fifty-over game, why not introduce a Twenty20 World Cup? Realizing it was too good an opportunity to miss, this was precisely what the ICC mooted in February 2006. Only the Indians and the Pakistanis protested, mainly because they hadn't thought of it first.

See also ONE-DAY INTERNATIONAL; SLOG.

TWINS

One of England's greatest mercies is that Don BRADMAN never had a more talented twin brother. Or even a less talented one, who might have developed a pathological jealousy of the Don, channelled all his fury into beating the Poms, and ended up AVERAGING only 80. Instead, the English had to put up with the Waughs, Steve and Mark, who became the first male twins to play Test cricket together, at Port-of-Spain in April 1991. Steve had actually made his debut five years before Mark, who was called up for the first time to take on England at Adelaide in January 1991. 'You're in,' Steve told him on the phone. 'Great,' said Mark. 'Who have they dropped?' 'Me,' said Steve. Mark hit 138, Steve was recalled a few months later, and in 2002 they were playing their 100th Test together. It was enough to bring a tear to the eye, particularly if you had been bowling to them for a decade.

The Waughs might have been beaten to it by Surrey's Eric and Alec Bedser had Eric's international career not been blocked after the Second World War by Jim Laker. The Bedsers would have become the first identical twins to play Test cricket, but that honour went instead to the Marshalls of New Zealand, Hamish and Justin. Their frizzy blond curls set them apart from everyone except each other, so spectators had to be on their guard at Auckland in March 2005 when Justin joined Hamish in the Test side against Australia and helped him add 38 for the second wicket. In a touching gesture of fraternal solidarity, both fell to Glenn McGrath for single-figure scores in the second innings.

But the first twins to play international cricket had already retired. Rose and Liz Signal represented New Zealand against England at Headingley in July 1984, which is just as well because they never got another chance. Rose made 0 and 8 not out, Liz scored 1, and neither took a wicket. It was Rose's first and last Test.

In fact, the Signals had very nearly been trumped by the Shevills. Fernie, who had married a Mr Blade by the time she played for Australia against England at Brisbane in the first WOMEN's Test in December 1934, almost lined up with her twin sister Irene, who missed out in that game but played in the next two. A third sister, Essie, appeared in all three matches. So you can imagine how Essie's *own* twin sister Lily must have felt when she failed to progress beyond the ranks of the New South Wales side. More recently, the identical Blackwell twins – Alex and Kate – played for Australia together for the first time against India in December 2004. 'We were fighting for the same position and I got used to living up to what she had achieved,' said Kate, fiddling nervously with a voodoo doll.

For sibling rivalry, however, nothing can quite match the Zimbabwe team that took on New Zealand at Harare in September 1997. For the first time in Test history three sets of brothers lined up in the same side: Grant and Andy Flower, Gavin and John Rennie, and Paul and Bryan Strang. Had Andy Whittall been promoted from twelfth-man duties to join his cousin Guy in the final XI, there would even have been a fourth set of relatives.

UMBRELLA

Two incidents at The Oval, separated by 123 years, show that this symbol of the English game has at times gone beyond the call of duty. During the gripping climax of England's 7-run defeat by Australia in 1882, the Test which gave birth to the ASHES, one spectator was said to be so anxious that he bit through the handle of his umbrella. Then, in 2005, with England needing only a draw to rectify sixteen years of urnlessness, sections of the Oval crowd began opening their umbrellas in unison in an attempt to fool the umpires that RAIN should be stopping play. The *Guardian* website's book on the series posed the ethical dilemma in its title: *Is It Cowardly to Pray for Rain?* 'Yes' was the only acceptable answer, swiftly followed by 'but who cares?'

UNDERARM BOWLING

Over 150 years before the daisy-cutter – the ball rolled along the ground – nearly caused a breakdown in diplomatic relations between Australia and New Zealand, it was the only action permitted by the Laws. The favourite explanation for the gradual rise of the bowling arm to above shoulder height begins with the Kentishman John Willes, who supposedly saw his sister Christina bowling round her body – with the arm parallel to the ground rather than perpendicular – in an attempt to circumvent her hooped skirt. In 1807, playing on Penenden Heath in Maidstone for Twenty-three of Kent *v* Thirteen of England, he decided to put this new round-arm action to the test. Predictably the tactic caused a rumpus, but it was not until fifteen years later, in a match at LORD's for Kent against the MCC, that Willes was repeatedly no-balled for an illegal action. He rode off in a huff, and never played cricket again.

But a revolution had been set in motion which the Laws were powerless to prevent. In 1828 the MCC permitted the bowling arm to be raised level with the elbow. And in 1864, 'overhand' bowling was legalized. These days the underhand version, known as the daisy-cutter or pea-roller or worm-burner or – Richie BENAUD's favourite, this – gazunder ('goes under'), is banned outside the confines of office cricket, where the need to protect the water-cooler and photocopier has given rise to increasingly inventive modes of attack. Willes would have approved.

In the twentieth century, the daisy-cutter only came out in exceptional circumstances. South Africa's Geoff Griffin took a HAT-TRICK against England at Lord's in 1960, but was also no-balled eleven times for CHUCKING. And when the sides contested an exhibition match after the Test finished early, he was forced to complete his over by bowling underarm after being no-balled yet again. Umpire Frank Lee promptly – and perhaps cruelly – no-balled Griffin one final time for not informing him that he was changing his action. And that, as far as Griffin's international career was concerned, was that.

Had Griffin's predicament taken place after 1981, he would not even have been able to use the underarm escape route. In a one-day game at Melbourne, New Zealand's No. 10, Brian McKechnie, had to hit Trevor Chappell's last ball of the match for six to TIE against Australia. But despite cries of 'No! No!' from Rodney Marsh behind the stumps, Chappell was ordered by his captain and brother Greg to bowl underarm: the batsman blocked the ball before hurling his bat to the ground. Daisy-cutters were quickly made illegal. 'I wish it never happened,' said McKechnie twenty-five years later in his 933rd interview on the subject. 'It still gets raised in other contexts, inside and outside of sport. When someone thinks Australia have done something to NZ they shouldn't have, the underarm comes up again.'

This might have been because the politicians became involved. The New Zealand Prime Minister at the time, Robert Muldoon, declared it 'the most disgusting incident I can recall in the history of cricket', although to be fair he had never witnessed Mike Gatting tackle a plate of Branston-pickle sandwiches in the Lord's pavilion; his Australian counterpart, Malcolm Fraser, called it 'contrary to the traditions of the game'. On 1 February 2006, entrepreneurs were still cashing in at a Trans-Tasman Business Circle LUNCH in Auckland to commemorate the twenty-fifth anniversary of the incident. Later in the year, a two-man play called *Underarm* opened in Palmerston North in New Zealand, examining – in the words of *The WISDEN Cricketer* – 'the angst caused in both nations by portraying a family with dual allegiances split by the furore'.

At the time, Greg Chappell defended his decision, claiming correctly that the Laws were on his side (yes, and they say it used to be legal for an inhabitant of Chester to shoot a Welshman with a crossbow if he was spotted inside the city walls after 11pm). But years later Chappell claimed that it came about because he felt he was losing his grip on the Australian captaincy: 'I was mentally wrung out, I was physically wrung out, and I was fed up with the whole system, things that seemed to be just closing in on us, and I suppose it was a cry for help.' It's an excuse that might be worth bearing in mind next time you find yourself advising your fast bowler with the opposition needing six off the last ball.

See also EXTRAS; GRUBBER; WOMEN.

USA

Until George W. Bush told an Indian journalist in February 2006 that he was a 'cricket match person', America's take on the sport has usually been summed up by the story of Groucho Marx's visit to LORD's to watch a county match. After a few hours, his companion (Michael Davie, the sports editor of the *Observer*) asked him what he thought. 'It's great,' said Groucho. 'When's it going to start?' In fact, cricket's relationship with the States began much earlier than any twentieth-century American would ever have imagined. The first Test between Australia and England at Melbourne in March 1877 is usually thought of as cricket's inaugural international fixture, yet the US and Canada had actually beaten them to it.

The story goes that in 1840 (or 1843, depending on which version you read) the St George's Club in New York were invited to Toronto to play on the shore of Lake Ontario. The invitation turned out to be a hoax, but the Canadians felt so sorry for their tired American guests that the two sides agreed to a game anyway. In 1844, the Toronto team was invited to MANHATTAN for a rematch. This time the American side was drawn not just from New

York, but also from Boston and Philadelphia, and crowd estimates range from 5,000 to 20,000. Around $100,000 was staked on the game, which the Canadians won by 23 runs inside two days after neither side managed to reach three figures in any of the four innings.

If there was some doubt over the status of the match – was it St George's *v* Toronto or USA *v* Canada? – then the first bona fide game between the two countries took place in 1853, which still beat Australia and England to it by twenty-four years. But cricket gradually gave way to baseball following the American Civil War (1861–65), during which soldiers on the Union side helped spread the game's appeal, and the fixture lost its lustre. When the two countries met at Fort Lauderdale, Florida, in the ICC Intercontinental Cup in May 2004, Asian and Caribbean ex-pats abounded. Even the Canadian-born John Davison, who took 17 wickets in the match to help his side to a 104-run win, had spent most of his life in Australia.

Davison had hit the headlines at the 2003 World Cup when he blasted a century off 67 balls against West Indies at Centurion – the quickest in the tournament's history – but the finest North American cricketer of them all was Bart King, who toured England three times between 1892 and 1921 with the powerful Philadelphian team; on the 1908 trip he AVERAGED 11 with the ball. How the USA could have done with him during the ICC Champions Trophy in 2004, when a team containing one player born in the States conceded 347 for 4 against New Zealand before being dismissed for 65 by Australia.

King would surely have been at home at the highest level, but by now the Americans were losing interest. They did not host a single FIRST-CLASS match between 1913, when the Australians visited Philadelphia, and 2003, when West Indies B played Guyana at St Croix in the US Virgin Islands. Not surprisingly, then, only two American-born cricketers have ever won a Test cap: Ken 'Bam Bam' Weekes, who played twice for West Indies against England in 1939, and hit 137 in 2¼ hours at The Oval; and Jehan Mubarak, the Sri Lanka batsman who made his Test debut in July 2002 and was born in Washington. Still, at least Groucho himself came close when John Arlott delved deep to describe the bizarre run-up of Pakistan's Asif Masood. 'He looks like Groucho Marx chasing a waitress.'

See also ASHES, THE; BEAMER; *TEST MATCH SPECIAL*.

V, THE

The classiest batsmen love scoring runs in the V, the unprotected area behind the bowler between mid-off and mid-on. It sounds like an obvious place to hit the ball, but it requires the precision of a surgeon or the power of a blacksmith or sometimes both at the same time. To score runs in the V is to demonstrate an almost innate affinity with the game and its aesthetics. It also proves that you spent your cricketing education listening to your coach, who was always screaming at you to play straight and show the full face of the bat to the bowler. Next time you're at a cricket match listen to the sound made by the crowd when a batsman drives a bowler straight back past him: an appreciative coo somewhere between admiration and awe. The noise might well have coincided with the appearance of one of the npower girls, but the chances are it was a natural response to one of the most satisfying shots in the game.

See also COVER-DRIVE.

WAGON WHEEL

A circular chart which catalogues the scoring areas of a batsman's innings, with each spoke of the wheel representing a particular shot. Fours and sixes are reflected by lines which run from the middle of the wheel – the pitch – to the edge; ones, twos and threes are correspondingly shorter. If wagons in the wild west had modelled their wheels on innings containing quick singles only, travel might have proved tricky. In fact, it's fair to say the Gold Rush of 1848 might never have happened. So it was fortunate that when Graham Thorpe made Test history by hitting only one four in a century against Pakistan at Lahore in November 2000, the wagon wheel was no longer the principal means of getting from A to B. Far more solid was the wheel produced by John Emburey, whose 46 for England against Tasmania at Hobart in December 1986 contained ten fours and a six. It was the highest FIRST-CLASS score to be made up entirely of BOUNDARIES.

See also NUDGE; NURDLE; SWEEP.

WALES

A small country west of England whose existence, in cricket's corridors of power, is a moot point: the England and Wales Cricket Board is habitually abbreviated to ECB. Glamorgan are the only Welsh team in the county championship, and their captain, Robert Croft, summed it up thus: 'Playing for Glamorgan is like representing Wales; playing for England is like representing the British Lions.' Except that England usually beat New Zealand.

See also RUGBY.

WALKING

Imagine a sprinter owning up to a false start or a boxer to a punch below the belt. Cricket, by contrast, has rarely had any qualms about its own moral standards, which is why the act of walking – whereby a batsman pre-empts the umpire's decision and gives himself out, usually caught behind or close to the wicket – has rumbled on into the twenty-first century. Derek Birley argues convincingly that walking is a by-product of the English class system: in the days when the distinction existed between amateurs and professionals, the largely public-school amateurs – almost always batsmen – would set themselves above the umpires in the pecking-order and therefore do their jobs for them. Far from being an act of sportsmanship, argues Birley, walking was a form of social one-upmanship.

These days, international cricket is played entirely by professionals, and the prevailing ethos is that the umpires should be left to do their job. Besides, argue the batsmen, enough players are given out when they should not have been, so why not stand your ground when you know you've NICKED it? It is a warped logic, but by and large it works – despite the fact that teams will think nothing of getting stuck into an opposition batsman for failing to give himself out when they know full well they would have behaved in exactly the same way themselves.

Problems can also arise when a player establishes a reputation for walking, then exploits the fact that the umpires regard him as honest. Some reckoned that the former England captain Colin Cowdrey would be happy to walk on 150, but less so on 0. Among modern players, Brian Lara routinely gives himself out, despite getting more than his fair share of rough decisions, while Australia's wicketkeeper Adam Gilchrist has broken with the traditions of his country by doing the same, most notably during the 2003 World Cup semi-final against Sri Lanka. On one occasion, he even proved too honest for his own good. When Australia played Bangladesh at Canterbury in 2005, Gilchrist marched off the field after apparently edging Tapash Baisya to first slip. But replays showed that the ball had merely flown out of a foothold at an odd angle – it had missed the bat completely.

Notorious non-walkers include W. G. GRACE, all of Gilchrist's compatriots, and Chris Broad. Once, during a Test at Lahore, Broad had to be persuaded to leave the field by his batting partner Graham Gooch after he was given out caught behind off Iqbal Qasim. Broad later became an ICC match official.

See also INITIALS.

WHEELIE BIN

Bowlers tend to object if they are referred to as anything other than gazelles (for seamers) or sorcerers (for spinners), so England's left-arm spinner Ashley Giles was particularly unimpressed to discover that TEST MATCH SPECIAL's Henry Blofeld had been describing him as a wheelie bin. Blofeld had borrowed the noun from the

*The wicket is easily disturbed. Here, a fielder tries to
sneak up on it without being noticed.*

Guardian's David Hopps, who was trying to convey the immense effort Giles had put in to taking 5 for 67 from 43.3 overs while struggling with injury during the second Test against India at Ahmedabad in December 2001. Giles, though, regarded it as a comment on his athleticism. '*Test Match Special* is all CHOCOLATE CAKES and jolly japes, but I didn't enjoy being called a wheelie bin, and nor did my family,' he protested, creaking a little.

WICKET

A wicket is a small GATE, so it does not take a giant leap of imagination to see why a set of three stumps with two bails on top should be so called. In fact, there used only to be two stumps, which these days would provide a get-out clause for umpires to explain to angry bowlers why they rejected their lbw appeal ('that was missing middle'). But a third stump was added in 1775 after Edward 'Lumpy' Stevens bowled Hambledon's John Small Snr several times without dislodging the bails. In 1931, the stumps grew an inch from 27 to 28, and in 1947 they had to measure 9 inches across rather than 8.

'Wicket' is also used to describe the pitch, when, strictly speaking, it shouldn't be. Everyone understands the usage, but that doesn't stop angry pedants flooding the *Daily Telegraph* with their letters. A wicket can also denote the demise of a batsman ('Smith lost his wicket when he was bowled neck and crop by Jones'), or a partnership between two batsmen ('the Waugh TWINS made grown Englishmen cry by adding 743 for the fifth wicket'). A walking wicket is a batsman who barely needs to set one foot in front of the other to give the impression that he isn't going to score many runs. During a village game in Derbyshire in 1938, both Kegworth and Diseworth made history by picking an entire XI of walking wickets. Set the grand target of 2 to win after restricting Kegworth to 1 all out, Diseworth were dismissed for 0.

See also LEG BEFORE WICKET.

WILLOW

Poor old willow. It's such a versatile wood, but there are a few otherwise perfectly reasonable human beings who believe its only use is to make bats and stumps and form part of that teeth-grindingly awful – and ever so slightly kinky – cliché about the thwack of leather. What would John Evelyn, a contemporary of Samuel Pepys, make of it all? In 1664, he wrote affectionately of willow trees: 'If we had them in greater abundance, we should haply grant the artifices who could employ them and the dexterity to vernish so neatly.' Presumably Evelyn was aware that Heliconian, the willow muse, was sacred to the poets, which is why Orpheus carried willow branches during his sortie into the underworld. Around Evelyn's time, however, scorned lovers donned caps made of willow twigs and leaves, and the wood has never lost its associations with sadness and melancholy. It is a tradition which was never more alive than when Chris Tavaré was at the CREASE.

See also ALUMINIUM; STONEWALL.

WISDEN

For many fans, the English season does not really start until they get their hands on the latest issue of *Wisden*

Cricketers' Almanack, one of the most famous sporting annuals in the world. Like a banana, it is yellow, chunky, compact and full of good things, most of them related to the previous year's cricket. It was founded in 1864 by John Wisden, a 5ft 6in ALL-ROUNDER who played for Kent, Middlesex and Sussex and who, in 1850, uniquely bowled all ten members of the opposition in one innings while playing for the North – despite coming from Brighton – against the South at LORD'S.

Since then, his book has gone from strength to strength: the first 1,500-page edition appeared in 1999, and its name rarely appears without the epithet 'the bible of cricket'. These days, the company also owns a monthly magazine (*The Wisden Cricketer*) and a website (www.cricinfo.com). In 2003, the one-off editor Tim de Lisle put a picture on the cover, thus relegating Eric Ravilious's woodcut of two men playing cricket in top hats to the book's spine. For some, it was as if a woman had been made Pope, but society's foundations steadfastly refused to crumble and the cover-shot has become a mini-tradition in its own right.

Wisden prides itself on its accuracy, integrity and independence, which makes the 'Errata' section one of the most entertaining reads in sports publishing. In the 2005 edition, for example, we learn that on page 539 of the 1978 book 'G. P. Howarth, not G. R. J. Roope, was the non-striker when J. H. Edrich reached his 100th hundred.' Quite how this glaring mistake was unearthed is not explained. Other, more famous, sections of the book include the 'Editor's Notes' (a high-class soapbox and an annual headache for the ICC), the 'Five Cricketers of the Year' (with the exception of Jack Hobbs, no one is named more than once), and the irresistible 'Index of Unusual Occurrences'

('County captain shins up tree', 'Warwickshire apologise to Somerset for announcer's "Wooooooooooh!"' – that sort of thing).

One of the most famous *Wisdens* is the 1939 edition, which Jim Swanton, the grand old man of cricket JOURNALISM for several decades, kept close by his side during his 3½-year stint working on the Burma–Siam railway as a prisoner of war. The book, he wrote, 'was the solace and in such demand that it could be lent out only for periods of six hours'.

See also CRICINFO; MASTER, THE.

WOMEN

For most of cricket's existence, women have been the gender that dare not speak its name, except when they are serving LUNCH or TEA. And while it is true that women do not bowl as fast as men, nor hit as far, the degree to which they have been patronized by their male counterparts has often taken the biscuit (a ginger snap, thanks, love). After Rachael Heyhoe-Flint captained an England squad consisting of nine teachers, four housewives and a secretary to victory in the first World Cup in 1973 (the first men's competition, note, did not take place for another two years), the MCC president Aidan Crawley grandly announced: 'You have done enough to deserve a game at cricket's headquarters. Welcome to the human race.' Actually, he didn't say that last bit, but then he didn't really need to. Women knew their place, and the only surprise was that they didn't come out to bat wearing aprons and brandishing rolling pins.

When women finally got the chance to play at LORD'S

in August 1976 – England beat Australia by 8 wickets in a one-day international – there were still caveats. Non-playing women were not allowed in the pavilion, and no women at all were allowed into the Warner and Tavern Stands, unless accompanied by a man (which was fair enough, really: they might have got up to all sorts). One MCC member, at thirty-one an old git before his time, was quoted as saying he was 'praying for RAIN. I couldn't believe this would happen in my lifetime.' Twenty-two years and much agonizing later, MCC members finally voted to allow women to join their club, although this might have had as much to do with the government threatening to withhold funds on the grounds of sexism as it did with a genuinely conciliatory approach to gender relations.

The decision came a mere 253 years after the *Reading Mercury* reported on a game on Gosden Common near Guildford 'between eleven maids of Bramley and eleven maids of Hambledon, all dressed in white. The Bramley maids had blue ribbons and the Hambledon maids red ribbons on their heads. The Bramley girls got 119 notches and the Hambledon girls 127.' The MCC's delay was also scant reward for Christina Willes, whose hooped skirt necessitated a round-arm action which persuaded her brother John that UNDERARM bowling should be a thing of the past.

The first women's Test took place at Brisbane in December 1934, when England's Myrtle Maclagan took 7 for 10 from 17 overs as Australia were dismissed in their first innings for 47. Maclagan hit a century in the second game, at Sydney, but her horizons were always broader than runs and wickets: her *WISDEN* obituary (she died in 1993 aged eighty-one) stated that at 'various times in her life she won prizes for squash, tennis, badminton and knitting', which makes Andrew Flintoff look like a one-trick pony.

Since then women have often struggled for funding and exposure – the 1973 World Cup took place largely thanks to a £40,000 donation from Jack Hayward, who went on to become chairman of Wolves FOOTBALL club – but these days they are taken more seriously. Not only do women now wear trousers rather than the faintly demeaning skirts which compromised their modesty, but they even staged the first TWENTY20 international, between England and New Zealand at Hove in August 2004. And now that the Asian nations have joined in the fun – India's women are referred to as the Eves – coverage in the media is better than ever. When Australia met India in the final of the 2005 World Cup at Centurion in South Africa, a decent number of cricket fans had heard of Karen Rolton, whose unbeaten 107 inspired Australia to victory (her one-day batting AVERAGE of 56 would have been gold-dust in the men's game).

Still, where there are women there will always be misogyny masquerading as chivalry. 'Did you know that Brighton College are playing girls in their First XI? Girls! I think it's absolutely outrageous,' spluttered Robin Marlar in 2005 shortly after taking up the presidency of the MCC. 'If there's an 18-year-old who can bowl at 80mph and he's been brought up properly then he shouldn't want to hurt a lady at any cost.' Clare Connor, the former Brighton College pupil who went on to win an OBE in 2006 for captaining England to their first ASHES win in forty-two years, described Marlar's comments as 'absurd, old-fashioned, and patronizing'. Some things, it seems, never change.

WONDERBALL

It all started when Shane Warne bowled Mike Gatting at Old Trafford in 1993. It was the 23-year-old Warne's first ball in ASHES cricket, and probably the most famous delivery in the history of the game (the 'Ball of the Century', reckoned the *Sunday Times*). It DRIFTED, pitched outside leg-stump, then spun back 18 inches to clip the top of off. Gatting looked bewildered, thinking for a moment that the wicketkeeper Ian Healy had knocked the bails off with his gloves. 'If it had been a cheese roll it would never have got past him,' observed Graham Gooch, his batting partner at the other end. But the truth is that whatever the filling in the imaginary sandwich, Gatting would not have got anywhere near it. This was the wonderball to end all wonderballs. The English press got excited when Ashley Giles produced the left-arm spinner's version to bowl Damien Martyn at the same venue in 2005, but the moment lacked the drama of Warne's entry.

WRISTS

In the real world, wrists belong to every member of the human race. In cricket, they belong exclusively to batsmen from the subcontinent, and, more specifically, to the Indian middle-order magician V. V. S. Laxman. If Laxman were paid a rupee every time his wrists were said to be made from steel or tungsten, he would now be the proud owner of a small island in the Indian Ocean. His genius lies in his ability to turn the wrists at the last minute and still get enough power on the ball to send it to the BOUNDARY. It is a skill that does not come as naturally to the predominantly white Test nations, who – so the stereotype goes – tend to rely on power and grit ahead of panache, and regard wristiness as effete.

See also ALUMINIUM; FOLLOW-ON.

WS, THE THREE

In the days before the world-wide web muscled in on the act, the three Ws meant only one thing. Well, three things actually: Clyde Walcott, Everton Weekes and Frank Worrell. Born in St Michael, Barbados, within eighteen months of each other, the three Ws made their Test debuts for West Indies in the same series (1947–48 against England) and were all, in their different ways, spine-tinglingly brilliant batsmen. All three ended up with knighthoods. Other than that, they had very little in common.

No one understood their significance better than the Trinidadian historian and journalist C. L. R. James. 'English people [. . .] have a conception of themselves breathed from birth,' he wrote in *Beyond a Boundary*, which many regard as the most intelligent sports book ever written. 'We of the West Indies have none at all, none that we know of. To such people the three Ws [. . .] help to fill a huge hole in their consciousness and in their needs.'

As batsmen they took up the West Indian baton from George Headley, who was known rather condescendingly as the Black BRADMAN. Between them they hit 39 hundreds in 143 Tests, and broke records almost for the hell of it. Weekes once hit five centuries in five Test innings, a unique feat that would have been even more impressive had he not been given controversially run out for 90 at Chennai when he was eyeing six out of six. Walcott, the most powerful of the three and an occasional wicketkeeper, scored five hundreds in a single series, against Australia in 1954–55. And playing for Barbados against Trinidad, he and Weekes once added an undefeated 574, which remains a record for any wicket in the West Indies.

Worrell was grace itself, and Neville Cardus felt he never played an 'ungrammatical' stroke. But more than the other two he affirmed the wisdom of the rhetorical question posed by James in his preface: 'What do they know of cricket who only cricket know?' When he was belatedly given the West Indies captaincy for the famous tour to Australia in 1960–61 following a tireless newspaper campaign by James, he was the first black man to hold the post. It was an appointment which united the Caribbean islands like never before, and it was no surprise when Worrell went on to become a parliamentary senator. Leukaemia cut short his life at the age of forty-two, but his standing was such that he became the first cricketer of any creed to receive a memorial service in Westminster Abbey. Today, West Indies and Australia still contest the Frank Worrell Trophy.

See also JOURNALISM; TIE.

XENOPHON BALASKAS (1910–1994)

OK, so technically he belongs under 'B'. And, granted, he isn't very famous at all. But he is included here to keep 'X-RAYS' company, and because his full name – Xenophon Constantine Balaskas – is simply too magnificent a gift for an A to Z to ignore. The son of Greek immigrants, Balaskas was born in the South African diamond capital of Kimberley, and – fast forward a few years – saved the most famous of his nine Test appearances for LORD'S. It was there in 1935 that he took 9 for 103 in the match with his LEG-BREAKS – what else would a man of his name bowl? – to inspire South Africa to their first win in England on a pitch 'ravaged by leather-jackets', according to *WISDEN*. His Test career was restricted by the war and a career in pharmacy, but surely the most disappointing aspect of his career was the fact that his nickname was 'Bally'.

X-RAYS

Whenever a batsman is hit anywhere other than amidships, the chances are that the team's press officer will gravely inform the media that he has been taken to the local infirmary for a 'precautionary X-ray'. Yet what else is an X-ray if not precautionary? This question is yet to be answered satisfactorily.

See also BOX.

YAHOO

Not the most elegant of shots, the yahoo is played with the head in the air and the eyes shut, and is best avoided should you have a history of back trouble. If the yahoo connects, the ball will either fly over the rope at cow corner or plop safely into the hands of a fielder, unless you manage to distract him while he is waiting for the ball to drop to earth. Yahoos are usually called 'wild', which is a typical cricket euphemism for 'downright irresponsible', and tend to be played by TAILenders or Shahid Afridi.

See also AGRICULTURE; SLOG.

YIPS

Such a little word, such far-reaching consequences. The sportsmen most commonly affected by the yips are golfers, who can inexplicably turn into cross-eyed, sweaty-palmed, jelly-legged gibberers at the sight of a three-foot gimme. But cricket has its own insidious form, which, for reasons that have never been adequately explained, tends mainly to afflict left-arm spinners. Grown men who have spent their cricketing lifetimes landing the ball on a good length suddenly lose their ability to do so, and end up sending down a mixture of LONG-HOPS and FULL-TOSSES while their team-mates look away in embarrassment. (If this happens to you on a regular basis, and you are fairly sure you don't have the yips, you are gently advised to take up another sport.)

Slow left-armers famously affected include Fred Swarbrook, who was reduced to rubbing a pebble given to him by a faith healer from Ilkeston and was eventually released by Derbyshire in 1979 after thirteen years' service. 'Only my wife has known what I went through,' he told Scyld Berry more than two decades later. Middlesex's Phil Edmonds was reduced to bowling off a couple of paces during England's tour of India in 1984–85 in what proved to be a successful attempt to cure his condition. And Ravi Shastri, of India and Glamorgan, describes the 'awful feeling' when he realized he did not know how to get the ball to the other end of the pitch. In his case, a month-long break from bowling did the trick. The response of New Zealand's Mark Richardson was to turn himself into an obdurate but highly successful opening batsman and stop bowling altogether.

More recently, two right-arm medium-pacers in county cricket have seen their careers disappear down the plughole. Yorkshire's Gavin Hamilton bowled five wides and a no-ball in his first over during a county match against Sussex in 2002 and asked his captain to remove him from the attack with figures of 1-0-17-0. 'He couldn't bring himself to bowl again,' reported WISDEN, 'and it proved to be his last over of the season.' Hamilton's haplessness had been hinted at a few years earlier when he won his only Test cap for England against South Africa at Johannesburg in November 1999: he was out for a pair and took no wickets in fifteen overs.

But at least Hamilton did not have to contend with the glare of the TV cameras during that career-defining match against Sussex. In the 2001 Cheltenham & Gloucester

Trophy final at LORD's, great things were expected of Leicestershire's Scott Boswell, who had dismissed a quartet of England internationals – Mike Atherton, Andrew Flintoff, Neil Fairbrother and Graeme Lloyd – during the surprise semi-final win over Lancashire. But in his second over in the final against Somerset he bowled a humiliating eight wides and was taken off with an analysis of 2-0-23-0. A month later, Leicestershire sacked him at the ripe old age of twenty-seven.

So why do the yips happen? Mark Bawden, who carried out research on the subject for Sheffield Hallam University, said: 'The bowler starts thinking about cricket skills that he hasn't thought about for years.' Other research has found that afflicted golfers use the analytical left-hand side of their brain more than the emotional and creative right.

Meanwhile, Dr Charles Adler from Arizona discovered in 2005 that golfers with the yips suffered from involuntary movements called co-contractions, or focal dystonia. These tiny muscle contractions are fine for understanding why that three-foot putt has at various stages been an ordeal of absurd proportions for world-class players like Bernhard Langer and Sam Torrance. But it cannot account for the sudden tendency of an experienced spin bowler to land the ball at his feet. No, in cricket the answer seems to be purely psychological, as if the bowler is objectifying himself rather than simply getting on with the job.

The message, then, is simple. The next time you are about to deliver that perfect away-SWINGER or cunningly disguised ARM-BALL, just make sure you do not, *under any circumstances whatsoever*, think about the batsman at the other end, or your team-mates, or the spectators, or even how foolish you will look if the ball ends up bouncing four times before it reaches the batsman. Avoid all those thoughts, and you'll be fine. Just fine.

See also EXTRAS; SLOWCOACH.

YORKER

In the days when W. G. GRACE's beard was more like bumfluff, to put Yorkshire on someone – or simply to york them – was to deceive them. Cricket pinched the shorter version and applied it to a very full-length delivery which sneaks under the batsman's defences and cannons into the base of the stumps. There is no more HAIR-raising sight in the game, with the possible exception of watching Arjuna Ranatunga attempting a quick single. The best yorkers are fast balls which SWING late and almost cause the batsman to lose his balance as he tries to dig them out. Very few Yorkshiremen other than Darren Gough can actually bowl yorkers these days, which is the kind of statement usually described in sporting circles as ironic (it isn't ironic; it's just a shame). For a true display of yorking, try Pakistan, where Wasim Akram and Waqar Younis used to pluck the delivery from thin air, and Shoaib Akhtar later bowled it at around 95mph, which is why it is also called the toecrusher, or sandshoe-crusher.

SHANE WARNE OFFERED TO SHOW ME HIS ZOOTER!

ZOOTER

In March 2004, Coca-Cola admitted that its trendy new brand of bottled water, mysteriously christened 'Dasani', came straight from the mains supply of one of the company's factories in Kent. But Shane Warne went one better. Together with his leg-spinning mentor Terry Jenner he concocted a delivery which became known as the zooter. It sounded exotic, but actually did very little other than go straight on. Still, that was not the point. The zooter – like the slider – existed to place uncertainty in the batsman's mind, not to bamboozle him in the air or off the pitch. This didn't stop people who should have known better from turning to each other every time Warne trapped another poor sap LEG BEFORE WICKET and saying wisely: 'That was the zooter.' No it wasn't. It was the one that didn't TURN.

See also FLIPPER.

INDEX

Note: Page numbers in **bold** refer to main entries